# THE ART OF
# DECISION
# MAKING

## BY RICHARD WORRINGHAM, PH.D.

**The Art Of Decision Making**
Copyright © 2000
Richard Worringham

ISBN: 978-0-9820180-3-3
First printing: 2008

**For information or additional copies, please contact**
Dr. Richard Worringham
440 Canterbury Ct. S.W.
Christiansburg, VA 24073
540-381-0746


Please visit my web site at
**www.sunrisepublication.com**

Printed in the USA
**by Morris Publishing**
3212 East Highway 30
Kearney, NE 68847
800-650-7888

# THANKS

This book would not have been written unless I had been blessed with three wonderful human beings, my children. As all children do when they are growing up, they wrestled with decision-making. In the process of nurturing them, I quickly discovered that parents also struggle vicariously with their decisions. It took me a while to learn that parents cannot make decisions for their children without undermining their autonomy. All parents can do is discuss the alternative choices, and leave the actual decision to their child. Of course parents will have opinions about whether the decision was the correct one under the circumstances, but this judgement should be kept to themselves. This is very difficult especially if the decision turns out to have negative consequences. There is nothing worse than making a mistake and then receiving a reprimand.

As a college professor, I learned a great deal from my students who came to me for advising each semester. At Iowa State and Radford University, all faculty were expected to advise a certain number of students each semester. With my help students negotiated course selection and registration, year after year, but sometimes, I was privileged to share problems relating to their personal lives, family relationships and professors! Their experiences, attitudes and insights were priceless!

Perhaps the hardest lessons I have learned as a father, counselor and pastor are these: in the style of Ecclesiastes, there is a time to intervene and a time to back off; a time to speak up and a time to listen carefully; a time to accept excuses and a time to push for accountability, a time to admit mistakes, and a time to try again. I say I have learned these things, but there is still room for improvement!

Last and by no means least, my wife Shannon and my daughter Megan have helped my writing with sage advice and eagle-eyed editing. In the process, they have tactfully practiced many of the lessons I mentioned above. I appreciate their help and encouragement.

# INDEX

# PREFACE

As a boy I found making decisions very difficult. Being blessed or cursed with an analytical mind, I often analyzed decisions to death. Unfortunately, I still came out of the process as frustrated as I began. Most of my frustration was caused by second guessing. The range of decisions was fairly wide and not limited to the profound. I mention this because the process of making a decision affects all aspects of our lives, from choosing an ice cream flavor to entering the Priesthood.

It was not only the making up of my mind that bothered me, but the persistent questioning afterwards. Am I doing the right thing? What will my parents think of me? Shall I propose marriage to this beautiful woman? What does God want me to do with my life? Should I remain in South Africa or go to America to pursue my dream?

I am not sure that I was ever quite satisfied with all of my decisions. Sometimes I regretted them, because I had committed myself to a mistaken course of action. Sometimes, I embraced my decision, even with serious misgivings, because it seemed I had no other choice.

The writing of this book was motivated by several concerns: first, I wanted to sort out in my own mind why I struggled with decisions, and to examine some of the factors that entered into them. Second, I wanted to share some of the insights I have gained over the years, and help readers see where they fit into the process. Third, I hope that leaders will learn to make better decisions, benefitting their lives, relationships and society in general.

My children, in different ways, and at different times, have exhibited all of the struggles I have experienced over the years. In fact, I have often wrestled vicariously with their decisions, even though they were their's to make! It is so easy to say, "I know what you are going through," but it doesn't help much, because no one can make decisions for them, and very few of the circumstances are ever identical. Sometimes when we do intervene, we may actually

i

rob that person of a very important learning process, the possibility of making a mistake. While we do not like making a mistake, I believe mistakes are good for us, *provided we learn from them!*

Decisions force us to discover who we are, what we want in life, and mostly, how to feel happy about important choices we have made. Despite what people think, we are not born with innate skills for making good decisions. I believe this ability is cultivated over time. We have to practice decision making over and over until it becomes an easier and more productive process. No one should be exempt from this process, because in many ways our maturity depends on it.

We should pay more attention to decision making in our family life and education. Education consists of countless decisions, for example, whether or not to go to school, whether or not to do our homework, whether or not to be punctual, whether or not to take notes, whether or not to ask questions, whether or not to prepare for an exam, and so on.

Decision making should also help us to be better citizens. In the USA, we take democracy for granted. Democracy is part of our heritage, and freedom to choose, a cultural ideal, but actually real democracy within our nation depends on whether or not we as citizens, make good choices. *Our government is only as good as the people we choose to lead it. Sadly, many do not exercise this right, but grumble when things do not go their way.*

At the risk of hyperbole, the destiny of the human race may well hang in the balance, unless we improve our skills in this regard. In the future we will need to decide how to eliminate terrorism, whether to use chemical, biological and nuclear weapons, whether to take global warming seriously, whether to use alternative fuels, how to conserve our environment, etc. Many of these are very urgent, and in some cases, life and death decisions. They are urgent because years from now the decisions we have made will affect future generations. Who will make these decisions and how will they decide? Others may, but we are not exempt from making them ourselves.

As I grow older, I realize that decisions are just as

important in my life now as they were when I was younger. Naively, I thought it would become easier as I aged, but it hasn't been easier, for a number of reasons. When I was younger, my life lay before me with many opportunities for mid-course corrections. Now, I recognize that time is running out, and the decisions I make are much more critical and final!

Decision making may well be the awesome consequence of being created in the image of God. I say awesome, because the freedom we have is amazing in its scope and implications. I believe that ultimately we will all stand or fall before an Eternal Judge, and the question that will be put to us will be: What did you make of your life and the opportunities you were given? What did you choose to do or leave undone in an incredibly beautiful world filled with many opportunities? Did you choose to live for yourself or others? Did you leave the world better off than you found it, or will others have to clean up the mess you made?

Even if you do not believe in God, you surely must believe that most decisions result in certain outcomes. We live in a world of cause and effect and many of them are predictable and relentless. Accountability, in a just world is, or should be, equally relentless. As men and women, we are accountable for our decisions. Do we acknowledge this responsibility, or do we blame others?

The "blame game" is a major problem in our society today. If it is not parents to blame, it is alcohol, or drugs, or police officers, or racism, or disease, or road rage, or religion or Satan. The truth of the matter is that no one can make us do anything. In most cases we are free to choose and do what we do. If we were forced to act against our will, then obviously, those that coerced us are to blame. Recognizing this makes a huge difference to our lives, because we often blame ourselves unnecessarily.

These are a few examples of the awesome scope of decision making in all its complexity. Hopefully, this booklet will help readers to sort out some of their thinking and bring about some acceptance and peace with the decisions they have made. Perhaps, it will make the future much brighter.

# INTRODUCTION

The Titanic was on its maiden voyage. It was touted as unsinkable, the safest and fastest vessel of all time. When the ship encountered icebergs, the captain was given a choice; stop and spend the night, or go on despite the danger. Stopping was obviously safest, but if the ship was unsinkable, the risk seemed minimal. The chance of establishing a record for the trans-Atlantic passage was attractive and so captain Smith chose to continue at twenty-two knots, right into a flow of icebergs.[1] As we know, the decision was disastrous and has gone down in history as arrogant and foolhardy. Was it? What would you have done in that predicament, if you had been the captain?

We all have to make decisions at one time or another, ranging from something trivial, such as what flavor of ice-cream to eat, to something really profound, like how to separate siamese twins! Decisions of the first kind usually don't require much thought, but decisions of the second kind exact agony of mind and heart. With the first, the only consequence might be a larger waistline; with the second, the consequences are irreversible. Clearly, the greater the risk, or outcome, the harder the decision is.

Most decisions are not debated in the abstract. They are usually found within specific environments and contexts of life which demand immediate attention. Nevertheless, decisions are motivated by a number of internal and external factors which may or may not be obvious to us at the time.[2]

Those who struggle with decisions envy those who make them with ease, but it's important to remember that both impetuosity and caution in decision making may have negative consequences. Ideally, we would like to have the best of both worlds, the "courage of our convictions" and the wisdom to "look before we leap!"

*The ability to decide is critically important to our development as individuals. At times it may literally be the difference between life and death!*

In the seventies, a rugby team was stranded in the snow capped Andes after their plane crashed. Starving with hunger, members of the team decided, very reluctantly, to eat the flesh of their fellow passengers frozen in the snow. What a terrible and disturbing decision, but the choice was either that, or death. No one, in the normal course of events, would sanction cannibalism, but given the situation, most people understood their decision. As a result of this terrible choice, a number of the men survived [3]

Not only do decisions convey a sense of power, but they are closely related to our self-esteem. In the example above, the first man to suggest that their dead fellow passengers might be a source of food, was afraid of what the others would think of him. Yet he knew that if they did not find some food to eat, they would die. Understandably, he also felt very guilty about his actions. He probably wondered how his family would react to him once they found out.

It is important to recognize that not to decide is actually a decision. In most cases, indecision relinquishes the power to someone else, and undermines our dignity. Over time this "abdication" of the power or right to choose, can be destructive to our mental health. Not only do we feel guilty about not acting, but we feel we have lost our value as a human being (our self-worth).

Guilt is often attached to decision making, both for making the wrong decision, and for failing to decide. While guilt may be regarded as a healthy and normal outcome, preoccupation with it can be debilitating and destructive. Some go over and over their decisions, examining them in minute detail. Generally, this guilty "second guessing" is counter productive, because once we have decided, there is very little that can be done about it. In most cases we cannot take it back and we must move on.

Roger was a young man who was never satisfied with what he bought. He would go on a buying spree, whip out his credit card and walk out of the store clutching several sacks full of clothes.

2

Once home, he would be embarrassed to bring his goods into the home. He would go through his packages one by one and feel guilty about his self indulgence. When the credit card bill came, he would feel guilty all over again because he had spent more money than he really could afford. Sometimes he would find satisfaction in returning the goods to the ever patient store......until the next time!

Jill was the designated driver one evening when she and her college buddies went out drinking. All except Jill, drank to excess and relied upon her to get them home. When the time came for her to do her job, her boyfriend would not give up his keys. After an acrimonious argument, she relented and let him drive. On the way home her boyfriend crashed head on into a car and killed himself and the other driver. Jill survived and carried with her not only a wounded body, but a very troubled conscience. *If only* she had taken the keys away or refused to get in the car, maybe it would not have happened.

A life cannot be taken back, but there is something that we can do to repair *some of the damage*. First, we may wish to pay restitution for the damage we have done. This is not always possible, however, and may be well beyond our means. Second, we may wish to obtain forgiveness or absolution from those we feel we have wronged. This also is not easy to accomplish, because even when we ask forgiveness, some people are not ready, or willing, to forgive. Nevertheless, *if we are truly sorry, and have made a genuine attempt to pay restitution and obtain forgiveness, we need to move on. As we move on, we will need to forgive ourselves, perhaps the most difficult of all.* It is at this point that the religious concept of grace has immense value. The belief that we are accepted and forgiven by God is a very powerful antidote to guilt and self-recrimination, *if we are willing to accept it. In this one thing (acceptance), we are sometimes our own worst enemies. We feel we must earn acceptance even when it is freely given.*

In the example of the drunk driver above, Jill called the parents of the boy and the family of the driver of the other car, and expressed her sorrow and grief. Though these encounters were very difficult, the families of the other victims were amazingly grateful that she had made the effort to contact them. Their positive reaction helped Jill overcome her guilt to some degree, as well as her unfounded fear of their hostile attitude.

Decision-making skills are usually cultivated over a long time. When we are children, most decisions are made for us by adults, but as we progress toward adulthood, we are expected to make more and more decisions on our own, and to deal with the consequences. Some say that taking responsibility for our decisions is the mark of maturity. This may be true, but it is an awesome task. No one likes to be involved in something that has the potential to haunt us for the rest of our lives. Some people are so afraid of making a mistake they are paralyzed at the moment of decision. It is not uncommon for a person in such a predicament to panic, avoid responsibility and even run away. Having the courage of our convictions (sticking it out, making it work) takes a great deal of courage. The belief that we can do it, despite the obstacles, is partly based upon our self confidence, and that is one characteristic that many lack.

*In my opinion, mistakes, the negative consequences of our decisions, are not bad in themselves, provided we learn from them, and do not repeat them over and over again. Sometimes, a failure can be healthy for us, because it can teach us more than a success, what not to do in the future.*

"The school of hard knocks" is a term which is often used to describe learning from bad experiences. The truth of the matter is that we can theorize and speculate and warn all we like, but until we actually experience the consequences of our decisions we will not learn very much.

The process of experiential learning is cyclical in nature can involve several cycles. In each cycle, there are basically four steps: first, we act with critical results; second, we look back retrospectively and analyze what we have done; third, we propose strategies for the future that will lead to change; and fourth, we try again.

Let me emphasize, that between each cycle there is an implicit need for change. If we do not change our behavior, we

4

have not learned from the past and will go on making the same mistakes over and over again, "spinning our wheels," as it were. Not all people learn from their mistakes as we might think, but most of us do, after one or two cycles!

Understanding why we behave the way we do, is key to our success. It may not eliminate bad habits that have been cultivated over time, but at least it may prevent similar mishaps. Once we observe a negative behavior, or recognize we have reacted in the same way, we must try to break the cycle. If we want improvement or success, it is essential that we develop coping strategies that prevent us from reacting in the same way as we did before and so enable us to move on.

No one likes to be corrected, but our openness to feedback about what happened is essential. Our assessment of the events may not be as accurate as we think, because we are too close to it to judge. In addition, feedback is not valued unless we trust the persons offering it, not always the case!

Being happy about the choices we make is probably the one thing that will bring us satisfaction and joy in living. Being satisfied with what we have chosen is an amazing gift. Very few people are perfectly satisfied with what they have chosen, one hundred percent of the time, but accepting a certain degree of satisfaction, say sixty to eighty percent, may be enough for us. What percentage is acceptable to you? This may be important for you to determine. Must you be correct a hundred percent of the time?

As I have said before, I believe decision making is an art that can be cultivated, it is not an innate gift or ability, as many think. We all have to learn this art at one time or another, and in fact our life may depend upon it! This booklet is about the art of decision making. The approach adopted is multi-disciplinary. It will draw from the insights of psychology, sociology and theology. To ground theoretical or abstract discussion, we will examine real-life situations and predicaments. For obvious reasons, names of persons involved in examples, have been changed to protect privacy.

# THE WONDER OF
# DECISION MAKING

Human beings have a truly remarkable ability to be reflexive. We can stand outside ourselves and examine our behavior and the roles we played in particular decisions. Such "objectivity" sometimes cannot be achieved without the help of a counselor or friend, who enables us "see" our behavior in perspective, but this ability is still awesome in its scope and implications.

The sweep of our decision making behavior, and responsibility for it, ranges across the whole spectrum of life, from the trivial to the profound (from entertainment to euthanasia, from parenting to international policy, from eating forbidden fruit to heaven and hell!).

According to the Book of Genesis, after creation had been completed, one of the first experiences of self-conscious human beings was loneliness. The second was the agony of decision making. As most people know, the dilemma that confronted Adam and Eve was the temptation to eat or not to eat the "forbidden fruit." This "moment" in the lives of humans has produced much scholarly debate and acrimonious discussion about free will, knowledge and responsibility. Some of it has even pitted the sacred and scientific communities against each other, which is most unfortunate.[4]

Regardless of our theological interpretations of this event, and its symbolic implications, it is clear that *one of the fundamental predicaments that early humans faced was the awareness that they had choices, and that choosing had major consequences for good or ill in their lives.* It was not just a decision to eat or not to eat; it was a decision to rebel despite strong warning, it was a decision to avoid confrontation (hide in the garden), it was a decision to blame someone else (Adam blamed Eve), it was a decision to avoid embarrassment (they discovered they were naked or vulnerable!), it was a decision to blame the serpent or the devil.

6

Any decision that affects our destiny, is awesome in its implications. Not only does it convey a profound sense of power upon us, but it implies great responsibility. Think about this for a moment; the Bible actually tells us that we have the power to rebel against the Creator of the Universe! Clearly, not all our decisions are that profound in their ethical scope, nor are we always able to assess the profound consequences, but we are usually aware that our decisions somehow affect our lives and the lives of others, temporarily and in the long term.

Whether at the dawn of history or our present day, we appear to be haunted by these inescapable decisions, though many would prefer to avoid them if they could. I believe that the *recognition that persons have profound choices to make throughout life, and that these choices affect relationships with others and their future destiny, is critical to our development.* In Greek there is a major distinction between time as it is measured ("chronos") and time as opportunity ("kiaros."). Of the two, the second is more important. We need to acknowledge that some decisions are pivotal moments in our lives and we need to make the most of them.

Not all of the so called "human sciences" hold that humans have absolute freedom of choice. Some argue that many factors determine the decisions we make, for example, heredity, genetics, environment, personality, peer pressure, family, religion, etc. If we allow for some of these influences in our lives, (which common sense suggests) it follows that we will quite often attribute (justify or blame) our choices to factors outside ourselves. We usually do not hesitate to attribute our *good* choices to ourselves, however. It is the *bad* ones we blame on others!

Attribution, or "the blame game," is a major problem in our society today. If it is not drugs or alcohol or parents, or television, or society, or genes, or fate, or the devil, *someone or something is responsible for our behavior, but not ourselves.* In the early church, the theological concept of being "born in sin" was often used to explain why human beings seemed incapable of doing the right thing. Unfortunately, even this concept, when carried to extremes, provides an excuse for our negative behavior: "I was born

7

in sin, therefore I can't help it".....I was tempted, and "the devil made me do it!" Are we ever accountable for our behavior?[5]

Today no one seems willing to be held accountable for the decisions he or she makes, and *maturity may consist of this: to take responsibility for decisions we have made, regardless of the many factors (conscious or subconscious) that may have influenced us.* Ultimately, "the buck stops here," as Harry Truman said, *and we need to face this fact with courage and conviction.*[6]

Some believe that the ability to make decisions is an innate or natural gift. People either have it or they don't. While this may be partly true, I believe decision making is a skill that can be learned and practiced from early childhood. It is a skill that should be stressed in our education much more than it is today.[7]

*One of the primary functions of parenting and education should be to teach children to make intelligent and satisfying decisions. Perhaps, even more importantly, people need to feel happy or contented with the choices they have made.* Those who are not taught these skills, often struggle in life, particularly when faced with major decisions and the guilt-laden consequences.

Decision skills remain with us all our lives and are either tarnished or polished by our relationships with others (our parents, peers, spouses, bosses, etc.) and the situations in which we live (family, playground, school, college, work, etc.). Sometimes, those who make decisions for us are regarded as "benevolent," "well-meaning," and "protective," but their "kindness" may actually be counter-productive. *Long term dependency on "well-meaning" decision makers, and the feeling of helplessness caused by it, can undermine our mental health and maturity.* Perhaps an example might help here.

In college, those who counsel incoming students, often encounter parents who want to make decisions about what courses their *adult children* should take in order to reach certain career goals. As an advisor in higher education, I have often come across this predicament:

Sitting across from Jeff and his father, it became obvious that the choice of major, and his career path, were his father's choices, not his own. Jeff was submissive and went along with his father's wishes. In diffidence to his father, he kowtowed to his every wish, but as time progressed he began to question his father's wisdom. In his senior year he began to rebel and seemed to be deliberately undermining his parent's plans by earning bad grades. Though his actions were probably subconscious, and obviously counter-productive, Jeff was asserting himself, even if the consequences were negative.

His father dismissed his behavior as "senioritis," a malady that affects many students near graduation, but there was more to it than that. It was necessary for Jeff's counselor to intervene in the situation, isolate him from his father, and ask him *what he wanted to do with his life, rather than what his father wanted him to do. He warned Jeff that unless he had a personal investment in what he was doing, it was unlikely that his decisions would be satisfying and productive.* His career hung in the balance. Telling his father what he had decided was incredibly hard for Jeff, but with the support of his counselor he was able to broach the subject.

Goal setting is a very personal and challenging task. No one can really set goals for us. We must decide what we want to do, where, when and how. A word of warning must be sounded, however, because some of the goals we set may not be realizable. *The truth of the matter is this: if we aim too high, we will fail, if we aim too low, we will be dissatisfied with ourselves. Nevertheless, it is better to set lower, more realizable goals and reach them, than to set higher, more unattainable goals and become disillusioned in our struggle to reach the impossible.*[8]

In Jeff's case, the situation was caught in time and turned out to be relatively harmless, but it is not always so. Sometimes decisions can be tragic and have long term consequences.

Consider a family in which there are abusive relationships. Here, submissive family members avoid decisions, or defer them, because it is too painful to question or disagree with a dominating spouse or parent. Over time, however, submissive persons feel trapped, frustrated and angry, but don't know how to cope with their inner rage and what to do about it.

Jim was a jealous and controlling husband who discouraged his wife, Margaret, from making any friends outside of the home. Though Margaret objected at first to the isolation and intimidation, and later, verbal and physical abuse, she was prevented from expressing her frustration to anyone outside of her relationship. Over time, resentment built but was overruled by fear. Eventually, after several incidents of physical abuse and demeaning treatment, Margaret decided to break free of Jim's control. She reported Jim's abuse to the police who took her husband away in cuffs. Margaret felt terrified by the consequences of her actions and desperately helpless. She assumed no one would believe her story and no one would help her. To her utter amazement, the police and courts were very understanding and sympathetic.

In such predicaments, breaking free is easier said than done. *Abused persons, who have been discouraged from taking initiative, find it excruciatingly difficult to make a decision to break free, and assert their independence. They require much encouragement, but once the decision is made, the consequences are profoundly beneficial.* Victims of abuse feels great relief and a restored sense of personal worth, dignity and power. Margaret adopted a significant acronym for her e-mail password, "IAWHMR ," which stands for "I Am Woman Hear Me Roar!"

*Neither over-protection nor extreme abuse are acceptable in family life and society. Normal and healthy relationships encourage, no, require that persons make responsible decisions and recognize the accountability that accompanies them. For healthy relationships to work, they must cultivate mutual respect, dignity and self-worth.*

The ability to make decisions is considered essential to professional life and leadership, but despite this awareness, there is much room for improvement in most walks of life. Strangely, decision making is not high on our educational priorities list, yet it may be the one factor that affects our lives the most. Consider these wider, political contexts:[9]

10

During the Second World War, the decision to build and deploy atomic bombs over Japanese cities was made by U.S. military commanders. Though the military scientists were aware of the power they were unleashing, they did not know what the actual toll in human suffering would be. The decision to deploy the bomb in Japan was rationalized by arguing that it would bring a long, protracted war to an end, and save many American lives. The achievement of "peace," was considered worth any human suffering that might occur. The bomb was dropped and the war was ended, but the devastation and suffering was indescribably more horrific and prolonged than they ever expected. Guilt for this act, directly or by association, has haunted most thinking Americans ever since. It may be this guilt or fear that ended the cold war and even today muddies the waters of our foreign policy with Iraq, Iran and North Korea.[10]

*Unfortunately, good decision making cannot be taken for granted. In some cases, inability to make quick decisions is looked down on by our society. An indecisive person is perceived as weak or ineffective, a decisive person is admired as powerful and influential.*[11] In most cases those in executive positions are the ones who make the decisions, but it does not necessarily follow that high ranking officials practice this skill easily or well. *History is full of great leaders who agonized over important decisions, and who were troubled with second thoughts after they had made them.*

Depending on our historic and political perspective, we have different attitudes toward the presidents of the USA. One thing is clear, however, most of them struggled to make up their minds! Abraham Lincoln agonized over the decision to declare war against the South. Not only did he pace up and down the White House floors, but he could not sleep and was in a state of continual depression. For months he could not decide whether to fire General McClellan or not, even though he knew his delaying tactics were counter-productive.[12]

Another of our presidents, Lyndon Johnson, struggled with decisions of war thrust upon him after the assassination of John F. Kennedy.[13] He inherited a legacy which not only plagued his office,

11

but scarred our nation to this day. As the Vietnam War progressed, and became mired in compromising guerilla campaigns, Johnson debated what to do. Should he commit more troops and equipment to the war effort, or withdraw gracefully? To escalate the war would alienate a growing number of American people: To negotiate a settlement would encourage Communism in the East. In the midst of his dilemma, he suffered terrible self-doubts and depression about his presidency. He did not seek a second term of office.[14]

The United States is one of the few countries in the world where freedom to decide is regarded as a fundamental human right and preserved by the Constitution. Americans believe democracy is impossible unless all people have the freedom to choose who governs them.

Even the economic system (Capitalism) that motivates most political decisions in the West, claims that manufacturers and distributers should be free to compete in the market place and that it is the right of consumers to choose one product over another. For this reason, monopolies in the USA are usually discouraged or deliberately broken up by the government.

Despite the high ideals of democracy and free enterprise mentioned above, there is buried deep in the psyche of most Americans an awareness that liberty and the right to choose is bought with a terrible price. The American War of Independence involved an audacious and risky rebellion against what was perceived to be a tyrannical and exploitative English motherland. The Civil War, which tore the country apart, not only concerned the freedom of the South, but the awful plight of enslaved African Americans. The U.S. entered the Second World War to free the world from the repressive regime of Hitler and the Third Reich.

In all these wars, paradoxically, there were those who were content to remain subservient under the jurisdiction and power of their leaders, even though they were aware of their ruthless and totalitarian practices! It is very hard for Americans to understand why people remain subservient to repressive regimes.

The assumption that all people will cherish democratic ideals seems axiomatic, but the fact is all human beings do not, and many citizens are quite content to allow their paternalistic governments to make decisions for them.[15] They are also content to allow themselves to be abused by authoritarian governments, to the point that they are incapable of breaking free. The "spiral of silence," a theory developed by Elizabeth Noelle-Neumann, may account for the gradual decline of free speech and democracy over time. Repressed people and organizations find it harder and harder to raise their voices against repressive regimes over time[16].

That many countries in the "developing world" are struggling to achieve democratic and stable economies after many years of colonial rule, is no surprise. Most colonialists believed that they alone had the right and ability to rule "backward and ignorant people." This paternalistic attitude kept the indigenous people out of leadership roles for many years. When freedom or independence was gained, many of the new governments faltered, because the people had not been taught to take initiative and make effective decisions on their own.

Recently, the United States chose to invade Iraq. It was alleged by President George Bush that Saddam Hussein was developing or producing nuclear, chemical and biological weapons. When the matter was debated in the United Nations, England sided with the United States, but France, Germany and a number of other countries decided not to support the war because they felt that there was insufficient evidence to justify it. Significantly, some claimed that the U.S. was an "autocratic" and an "imperialist" bully, and that the champion of freedom had become an oppressor.

Mr. Bush, on the other hand, rejected these negative characterizations, claiming that the United States only wished to remove an autocratic leader and establish a democratic government in Iraq. Unfortunately, this democratic ideal has been undermined by growing sectarian violence. The protagonists do not seem to respect their present government because they believe it does not represent them adequately, and it seems incapable of stopping the violent clashes that occur almost every day.

Those who oppose the war in Iraq believe that as long as our troops are there, the nascent government will never rule with confidence and establish law and order. *Ultimately, the people must decide if they want to be ruled by democracy or theocracy.* Most Americans do not understand this because their culture conveniently separates church and state.[17]

In the future, the peace and prosperity of the world may hang on how many countries do, or do not, value democracy, and which do, or do not, promote freedom of choice in politics, economics and religion. Democracy is vulnerable wherever people do not exercise enlightened decision making or fail to elect representative governments. *There is an urgent need for decision making skills to be learned and applied at all levels of life, personal, family, community, nation and world. We have a long way to go before this wonderful gift is exercised by all human beings, equally well, everywhere.*

Indeed, the freedom to decide is an awesome responsibility which humanity is still learning to exercise. It is also evident that even those who espouse democratic ideals have much to learn themselves!

# INTERNAL AND EXTERNAL FACTORS

Though it is important to take responsibility for our decisions and actions, and maturity may be gauged by our willingness to take the blame, it would be foolish to deny there are many extenuating factors that influence and affect our decisions. Many of these are simply not our fault and we should not be held accountable for them. How can we distinguish between the two? When are we to blame and when are we not to blame? As we will see later, guilt and responsibility can become terrible burdens, if they are not dealt with.

Extenuating factors may be roughly divided into internal and external. External factors include the situation in which we find ourselves, our culture, family background, peer group, religion, culture, social mores, and so on. Internal factors include genetics, our personality, self-esteem, our sense of confidence, feelings of insecurity and vulnerability, etc.

Despite the fact that some of his work is viewed with skepticism by many scholars, Freud's concepts of psychoanalysis can help us to understand the complex relationship between internal and external influences in our lives. Though our conscious minds enable us to identify and describe external influences, we are not always aware of subconscious ones. Our unconscious minds are a reservoir of feelings thoughts and memories which can be very painful and conflicted. Though the "ego" is largely unconscious, it prevents us from acting out basic urges, needs and desires which are created by the "id." If it had its way the "id" would give in to urges, needs and desires without regard to the "ego" and the "supper ego." The "ego" tries to keep a balance between our moral or idealistic standards and reality. The "super ego" consists of internalized ideals which we have acquired from our parents and society. The "super ego" suppresses the urges of the "id" and tries to make the "ego" behave morally.[18]

15

Despite the bromide "ignorance is bliss," what we don't know may be more troubling than what we do know. Identifying the factors that influence our choices can be helpful, not only because they partly explain why we choose what we do, but because they reveal hidden biases, tastes, and values. As we have seen from Freud's analysis this may not be as easy as we think. We may not know our minds, or understand ourselves, as well as we imagine that we do. Later, we will consider several external and internal factors in detail, but for the moment let us examine a few examples:

One of the marks or characteristics of life, especially in the West, is the increased pace with which we do things. Everybody seems to be in a great hurry, and as a result, rapid decisions are becoming more and more essential to our survival. The pressure of a "fast-paced life" is accompanied by impatience with ourselves and others, because we cannot make decisions quickly enough and easily enough to suit our life-style. Some suggest that the computer is the answer to this inability and there is no doubt that many decisions are made quickly and efficiently by means of it! Some are not too sure of the computer's contribution, however, bemoaning its invention and the impersonal nature of speedy transactions. It is interesting that as each generation of a computer is produced, manufacturers claim that it is faster than its predecessor. Users also complain about how slow their old computer is in comparison with the new one. Actually, it is not the speed of the computer that often proves to be the problem but rather the users adaptability!

Think for a moment about a motorist waiting in a line of cars, entering a freeway. By definition a freeway implies great speed, but it is typically the entry and exit ramps that provide the greatest difficulty for us. Some motorists are very cautious and wait interminably for the right moment to enter traffic. Others gun their motors and enter the flow of traffic after only a few seconds of hesitation. The first kind of motorists shake their heads at the risk-takers, the second shake their heads at the slowpokes! Technologists brag that computer-controlled traffic lights and timed entries will solve the problem, but those who hate computers complain that humans are handing over more and more of their decisions to inanimate devices. They prefer the friendly traffic cop! From this example, it is clear that there are pros and cons for excessive caution or extreme confidence in decision making. Neither procrastination nor impetuosity are considered good virtues and probably there is room for some compromise, or middle ground, between the two extremes!

Making good decisions is hard work and demands a lot from us. Those who make impetuous or quick decisions usually do not like analyzing alternatives and exploring possibilities before they make their move. They prefer to do things on the spur of the moment. This spontaneity reduces the agony of the decision and gets it over quickly with less effort. *Though spontaneous and impetuous people experience less agony in the decision making process in the short run, they may feel dissatisfaction with the results of their choice in the long run.* Notice the proverbial wisdom contained in the saying: "Marry in haste, repent at leisure!"

More cautious or methodical persons, on the other hand, may do the research, weigh up pros and cons for days, and prioritize the issues involved. *Though this may be an agonizing process, initially, the chances are that the choice will provide more satisfaction for them in the long run.* Notice again the proverbial wisdom: "more haste, less speed."

Impetuosity or spontaneity is often associated with mood. We *feel* right about it at the time, or we do not. Since moods are ever changing, the foundation of this kind of decision-making is obviously not very reliable. *In retrospect, we may often recognize that our decision was based upon how we felt at the time and nothing more!* Most people are aware that sometimes their feelings can run counter to their rational judgement and they regret their decisions bitterly.

Because of a bad childhood experience, I know a woman who has a strong fear of wasps. Her instinctive reaction when she sees one, is to get away from it, as quickly as possible. She confided that one day a wasp was trapped in a car in which she was traveling. Her fear was so strong that she requested the vehicle be

17

stopped immediately. *Failing that, she was actually contemplating jumping out of the moving car!* Most would judge this phobic reaction as irrational and in fact, the woman will readily admit that her feelings are irrational, but her emotional response overrides her rationality and she feels compelled to get away. Some therapists have found that phobias of this kind can be overcome with a "flooding process" in which the person is exposed to the troubling situation or experience over and over again until a degree of calmness and rational control is reached.

Ignorance about our fear of decisions may cause misunderstanding, discomfort and hesitation, all of which may be misinterpreted by others. Consider the following complex relationship and the misunderstanding that occurred.

Judy and Bill met through e-mail and started dating. Bill was a Protestant, and Judy a Catholic. Though they were well-suited and happy, a critical moment in their relationship arrived as their desire for sexual intimacy increased. For Bill, sexual pleasure demanded immediate, spontaneous gratification, but Judy hesitated. She was not sure if Bill would think she was cheap and easy. Would he respect her as much after sexual intercourse, as he did before? As a Catholic, Judy believed sex was on the level of a sacrament, and should be sanctified by marriage. She questioned whether their relationship was just lust or the beginning of a long-term, loving relationship. Commitment of this kind raised several questions in her mind. Did they really love each other deeply? How compatible were they? Should they wait until they knew each other better? What would her parents think if they found out she was sleeping with Bill? If they had sex, should they use contraceptives? If they had unprotected sex, what if she fell pregnant? Note that *all* of these "apparently fearful" questions were precipitated by and related to one decision; to have or not to have sexual relations. Clearly, Judy's values were deeply embedded in her mind, but Bill had a hard time understanding why she hesitated.

At the risk of being stereotypical, most males find hesitation on the part of a woman, and the numerous questions associated with it, as a sign that a woman does not really love them. They will actually use this argument ("Your hesitation shows me that you really don't love me") as a weapon of persuasion to get what they want. Women tend to be more cautious because, typically, they are the ones who have more responsibilities and have to live with the consequences of their decisions (pregnancy). In an effort to overcome their hesitancy, women will often overrule their natural and legitimate caution, to prove that they really love their partner. Such impetuosity may not be normal to them and they may regret it later.

*Sadly, it was not because she did not love Bill that Judy was hesitating, but because deep in her mind she was wrestling with a number of issues that needed to be resolved before she made the decision to be intimate.* She was afraid of the multitude of implications that this one act would precipitate. It is critically important that both men and women understand this. Hesitation and dissatisfaction with a major decision can be a sign that a number of major underlying issues have not been resolved. Unresolved issues, typically, are also the source of regrets and second-guessing.

Obviously, there is a need to communicate what is going on inside of us (if we can) or mention what factors outside of us we find troubling. It is not enough to identify them in our thinking, we must try to articulate them, "share them," so that others involved understand "where we are coming from." To do so may be risky, for there may be some factors we would not like to mention or are ashamed about. To tell or not to tell, is in itself a decision. What we fear is that the truth will jeopardize our relationship or that the person or persons will not understand. It is critically important to trust the person in whom you confide.

Personally, I believe that the truthful path is always the better one, but if people are not mature enough to handle it, then perhaps they are not the kind of people that will enjoy deeper and more satisfactory relationships with you. *As a general rule, candor should only be used if you have established security and trust over time. Without these, it may be very foolish.*

# FEAR OF MAKING A MISTAKE

*Probably the primary or most powerful reason why people find decisions difficult, is the fear of making a mistake, and the imagined negative consequences that might be associated with it.* In a society that is preoccupied with success and the goals that reach it, our choices are critically important. Depending on our attitude and the attitude of others, we may perceive mistaken choices along the way as failures or weakness.

An example may help to illustrate this. Most degree programs have courses arranged in a sequence, and some courses have certain prerequisites. A wrong choice at registration time can result in a sequence of unfortunate events, denied access to classes, delay of a whole semester, and even postponement of graduation. Most parents expect their children to graduate in three years, and failure to do so can be devastating. For this reason some senior students request that their course selection to be confirmed several times. Doing an "extra" or "unnecessary course" may be considered a serious mistake, but sometimes the additional knowledge can be beneficial!

At the risk of overemphasis, it is important to recognize that *making a wrong decision is neither a weakness nor a failure*, provided it is followed by three things: one, recognition that successful persons can make bad decisions; two, learning from mistakes is a strength not a weakness; and three, walking away from mistakes with determination to do better, is sign of courage. Failures are only bad if we are preoccupied with them and allow them to haunt our lives, preventing movement onward.

In some cases, the consequences of a decision may be irreversible and we may have to live with them, but in many cases they are reversible. People are much more willing to accept those who own up to mistakes, particularly if they have learned from them, and have the courage to try again. They are not so willing to

20

accept those who deny responsibility, blame others for their predicament, or wallow in self-recrimination.

One of the possible reasons for the fatal decision of the Captain of the Titanic was his desire to break a transatlantic speed record. The decision was also based upon the mistaken belief that the ship was unsinkable. Though both of these motivations were flawed, and the result disastrous, the sinking of the great ship was had positive outcomes. Ships in the future were equipped with sufficient lifeboats, twenty-four hour radio operation, sealed compartments, a higher grade of steel plates, and so on. Yes, this was a costly mistake that shook the world's confidence, but the mistake brought many benefits and improvements as a result.[19]

Closely related to the fear of making a mistake is a sense of guilt. Most of us do not like feeling guilty and one way of avoiding guilt is to postpone the decision that produces it. It is important to recognize that guilt usually occurs when we blame ourselves for past mistakes. Reliving the past is fairly common, but reprimanding and punishing ourselves repeatedly, is not healthy. Again, *it is critically important to take blame only for those decisions or actions for which we are truly responsible.* To do otherwise is really unnecessary and self-destructive. Of course, this is easier said than done, but an attempt must be made to limit culpability.

In religion, guilt can often be removed, through a process of confession, forgiveness, reconciliation and assurance. Admitting that we were wrong, and that our wrongs have hurt others, is a difficult thing to do, because many people are too proud ever to admit these things. Forgiveness is the gracious gift of those who have been hurt by our wrongdoing. It is critically important to recognize that forgiveness cannot be bought or manipulated. It must be given freely. *Reconciliation between victim and perpetrator can only occur when there is mutual acceptance and the renewal of a trusting relationship.* Sometimes, trustworthiness comes only after a prolonged demonstration of credible behavior on the part of the perpetrator.[20] Despite the process mentioned above, guilt will not be removed, if we constantly remind ourselves of the wrong that we have done, *and fail to accept forgiveness and forgive ourselves.* It is a paradox of life, that even when we know we are forgiven, we still go on punishing ourselves.[21]

The fear of making a mistake can also be accentuated by perfectionism. A perfect person, by definition, does not make mistakes.[22] Of course it does not matter that there are no perfect people in existence, so long as we hold ourselves to this standard! Much suffering in life is caused by people who believe that they are perfect and are contemptuous of those who are not. Once we understand that we are not as perfect as we think, and that others are not perfect even if they think they are, we are more likely to accept a few mistakes! It is vitally important in religion to understand that though God may be perfect, He does not expect human beings to be perfect before He forgives them. Christians believe that Jesus is their mediator and advocate and that He offers His perfect life on our behalf. This Divine initiative "covers" or "masks" our imperfection.

Perfectionism is also negatively related to risk-taking. All decisions involve some degree of risk, but most people feel uncomfortable with taking risks. Exploring an infinite array of options or possibilities might seem a logical way to minimize risk, but who can possibly take the time to do this? There is an element of risk in everything we do. What is more helpful for us, is to decide what level of risk we are prepared to handle or tolerate, and move on.

A lack of data can also postpone a decision. No one will deny that it is wise to delay a decision until there is enough information. Obviously, the more we know before and after a decision, the better the decision will be, but how much knowledge is enough? How much data do we need, and how certain do we have to be, before we decide?

The possession of complete knowledge is humanly impossible. Maybe this will change when we get to Heaven! St. Paul hoped for just such a condition when he wrote, "in this life we see puzzling reflections, but in the life after death, we will see clearly, face to face!" *Until then, we simply will have to accept the level of knowledge we have, and act upon it. Our knowledge will never be perfect in this life!*

For this reason, an element of "faith" or "trust" is essential to decision making. When we have "done our homework," and explored most of the possibilities, there comes a moment to decide. *If we have been truly conscientious, we must move on, trusting that we have done the best we could under the circumstances, We cannot go on waiting for the perfect moment or answer, we must step forth in faith, we must decide. Even if the decision is ultimately wrong, that does not matter; it was a "good-faith decision."*

Another fear associated with decision making is caused by the preoccupation with the consequences of the decision. Most of us have fertile imaginations which allow us to explore all sorts of possibilities. Unfortunately our imaginations can be over-active and may need to be curbed. A reality check with a friend or confidant will help bring us down to earth. He or she may help us determine how predictable the results we fear may be.

Perhaps a few examples may help illustrate the theoretical discussion above. Recently, the explosion of one of the Space Shuttles on re-entry shook our nation. Naively, we all believed that NASA could do nothing wrong. After all, there had been so many successful launches and landings. In the aftermath of the explosion, many wanted to ground the Shuttle until *all* the problems could be solved, which would take a long time. Surprisingly, many of the astronauts wanted to fly again as soon as possible, because *they recognized that every flight they took had an element of risk in it. If they were to wait for the perfect spaceship, they would never take off. They were prepared to accept a certain degree of risk and live with it.* [23]

Sally was in a disintegrating marriage. She was a good mother, but every time she and her husband, Jack, quarreled the issue of divorce came up. Jack would criticize her parenting skills, threaten to report her to the social welfare department, say he would take her children away from her, and systematically destroy her life. No mother wants to lose her children. Sally began to doubt whether she was a good mother and to feel guilty about her failures. She wondered if Jack had evidence against her, or whether he was just "blowing smoke." Would the court find in favor of Jack and give him custody of the children? She could not bear the thought of that. Many days later she discovered that Jack was indeed "blowing smoke" and that her fears were actually groundless. For a long time, Sally was imprisoned by her over-fertile imagination, unnecessary fears and a large burden of guilt, and her husband knew just how to exploit them!

Over-estimating a person's power, and a husband's ability to do harm, is very common and is usually sufficient to keep a wife submissive in an unhealthy relationship. It is vitally important to discover what the truth is, and to fully understand how real the threat or the consequences are.

From the examples above, it is clear that we need to be careful of playing the "what if.....game." We all play this game at one time or another. What if you have a stroke? What if the stock exchange crashes? What if global warming floods our city? What if our enemy uses its atomic bomb capabilities? *Conjuring up all sorts of unpleasant outcomes in our mind is easy to do, but how realistic are the imagined events or consequences? Can our prognostications be demonstrated specifically, or are they figments of our imagination? We must try to develop reliable tests to gauge how likely anticipated outcomes are.*

Prognostications should be as accurate as they can be, given our knowledge, otherwise they are a hindrance. What is the evidence from our research? What do the authorities say? Is there any doubt? Can we draw such conclusions from the data? There are many events that might occur in the future that *are beyond our prophetic skills to predict, or our ability to control. We may be able to calculate the chances, but in most cases, sadly, we have to deal with the consequences when we get there!*

Addressing the uncertainty and unpredictable nature of life, Jesus said, "sufficient unto to the day is the evil thereof!" This philosophy or theology is echoed in the Alcoholic's Anonymous' goal for sobriety "live one day at a time." This may be paraphrased as, "be accountable for short and immediate portions of our life and not the whole of it. Such brief moments or opportunities are much more manageable than long-term ones.

# THE PARALYSIS OF
# DECISION MAKING

As we have seen, there are many reasons why people fear the processes of making decisions. Unfortunately, the fear is so great that it paralyzes us. How can we overcome this paralysis?

Reflexively, many stand between the past and the future, incapable of moving forward because they cannot make up their minds. Let us examine some of the factors that thwart decision making and result in paralysis.

We have recognized that sometimes there is not enough information on which to base a decision and we are uncertain about all the possible consequences. In this predicament we tend to postpone the decision, hoping that something or someone will provide us with better insights. How long will we wait? If we wait too long, we may be simply allowing "fate" (animate or inanimate forces outside ourselves) to decide for us. Of course, nothing significant may ever happen, and we will spend all our time "spinning our wheels."

*In most cases, data will not become available unless we seek it out. We must get out of our passive role and take some initiative. Not only is this good science but it is good psychology.* Many people retreat into their minds and speculate inwardly. The real danger is that limited input will cause us to find simplistic solutions and undermine our arguments. We need to get out and work at gathering data. We need to broaden our perspective.

Where can we find more information? We will need to consult others. We will need to find authorities, professionals and experts to guide us. We may need to share their experience and even participate with them in their work. If we are students, we may try to discover if there are internships available. We need to determine what others have done in the circumstances and how they have succeeded or failed. An example might be helpful here.

Susan applied to several graduate colleges. She was very pleased to find that four colleges were interested in her application based on the essay she submitted and her undergraduate record. These positive responses were pleasing to her, but overwhelming. Now, she did not know how to choose between the many colleges! She could wait and see if the colleges contacted her again. She could wait for her GRE scores; the results might determine which colleges would accept her and which would not. Waiting patiently might be considered appropriate, but there were other things that she could do in the mean time.

Susan sought additional information from the colleges, wrote to find out if GRE scores were the sole criteria for admission, visited the colleges to meet with her future professors, and took several tours of their college campuses. Not only did this activity keep her busy while she waited, but it gave her a context within which to place each application. With this additional knowledge, she was able to decide more intelligently between them when the results came.

Another consequence of passive decision-making, or paralysis, is allowing others to make the decision for us. While this is somewhat better than relying on the circumstances of life to determine our destiny, it is actually unfair and dangerous. It is unfair because we are abdicating our willpower to another, and if anything goes wrong, we can always blame them for our trouble. Waiting for persons to make decisions for us, and accepting the outcome, is hardly a decision. We are actually subjecting ourselves to another's will; perceptions, desires, prejudices and all. It is also dangerous because we are vulnerable and can easily be exploited if the person does not have our well-being at heart. Let me give another example.

Paul worked for a successful telecommunications firm. He was good at his job and well liked by his boss. Most of his fellow workers had received raises, but Paul had not. He wondered if there was anything wrong, but was too afraid to broach the subject or ask for a raise. He simply could not bring himself to approach his boss, *partly because he believed* that *it was his boss' responsibility to notice his excellent work ethic and reward him accordingly.*

Unbeknown to Paul, his boss was actually waiting for him to take the initiative to come in and discuss his future with him. Because nothing happened, Paul became discouraged, his work suffered and eventually he handed in his resignation. In his exit interview, the boss asked him why he was quitting. He reported that he had not received a raise and felt unappreciated. The boss replied: "You never asked for a raise!" *Paul blamed his boss for failing to recognize his efforts and reward them,* but he could have taken some initiative, and asked for one. Taking initiative is critically important and is often used as a criterion for hiring and promotion. Why didn't Paul take the initiative? The worst outcome that could have occurred, if he had taken initiative, was being turned down. At least he would have known where he stood.

While passivity can thwart decisions, so can hyperactivity! One of the marks of modern society is the over abundance of information and potential choices. Too much information can overwhelm us and make it difficult to "see the forest for the trees." It is necessary for us to reduce information to the essential minimum to avoid being overwhelmed.

A highschool student, Alan, was trying to decide on a future career. His career guidance counselor suggested that he search the Internet for job openings under certain categories, and take an aptitude test to determine what careers matched his strengths and interests. To his amazement the computer's listing included five hundred positions that suited his profile. Among others, the test revealed that he would do well at teaching, nursing, counseling, medicine and ministry. *Alan was overwhelmed by all this data. His decision had become harder, not easier.* He needed to reduce the amount of information to a workable minimum.[24]

In other research, Alan discovered that careers in medicine and nursing required a good background in mathematics and science (not his strong suits). Ministry was interesting, but he was not a member of a local church. He would have to establish some record of involvement in specific kinds of lay ministry before most boards of ordained ministry would even consider his application. Knowledge of preparatory backgrounds and requirements, reduced his choices to a more reasonable level.[25]

Procrastination is another form of passivity that thwarts decision making. We find all sorts of reasons to avoid doing what we know we have to do. Ultimately, time forces us to make the decision. Putting off decisions to the last moment is easy enough to do, if a dead line is way off in the distance, but if we wait until we have reached the deadline, we are opening ourselves to some serious risks. *Last minute decisions are hardly ever good ones, because they are usually made in haste, or under great duress. It is better to set timetables or intermediary goals before the critical moment arrives.* Such activity, not only keeps us on track but gives us a sense of accomplishment. When the deadline arrives, we are ready for it.

Peter and Julie were very much in love and contemplating marriage, but were cautious about setting a date and planning their wedding. Whenever his fiancé raised the subject, Peter put off the subject, reasoning that he had plenty of time to make up his mind. Though he was a member of the National Guard he felt sure that his unit would not be called up and sent to Iraq. Then, an official letter arrived in the mail indicating that his unit was indeed being sent to Iraq and that he had to report for duty in two weeks. Suddenly, everything changed and the couple decided to get married before he left. The hasty marriage plans eliminated many of their romantic dreams and plans and they admitted afterwards that their marriage was an anticlimax, if not a mistake.

# NOT TO DECIDE IS
# TO DECIDE

We have seen that some people believe that decisions can be handled simply by doing nothing. They believe the situation will either solve itself on its own, or others will deal with it. Mistakenly, we think that such passivity absolves us of all responsibility. We reason that we can hardly be blamed if we did not choose a course of action? No, actually, the choice to do nothing *is a choice with attending consequences.* It is for this reason that many counselors practice "non directive counseling" in which they help their clients to understand their predicament, and make appropriate decisions for themselves. The counselors are reluctant to tell their clients what to do because they open themselves to blame. *The client can say, "You told me what course of action to take and look what happened!" Actually the clients are still accountable, because they gave up their decision making ability and trusted someone else to decide for them.*

Choosing to do nothing is a form of abdication. We decide to let others make the decisions for us. *Smugly, we may rationalize that if we didn't contribute to the decision making process, we have the right to criticize those who did!* There are several problems with this. Unless we know who it is that takes our place or stands in for us, we can open ourselves and others to all sorts of abuse. If we are lucky, the person may be well-meaning and noble, but sometimes the person is not. The recognition that we did nothing, when we had the opportunity, elicits powerful feelings of guilt. Whether we like it or not, there is an element of complicity. Two examples may be helpful.

When Hitler introduced the "final solution" (the eradication of the Jews in death camps) there were some Germans who were ignorant of what was happening, but there were others who knew about it and did nothing. Those who claimed ignorance may be given the benefit of the doubt and judged innocent, but what about

# CEREC® 3D

1-800-873-7683

My Friend Chris,

I respect And love
You man.

Thank You for letting
me visit.

Washed I washed the
blankety pillow I used.

Your Brother,

those who knew and did nothing? Were they innocent? Why didn't they stand up and oppose the Gestapo? Why did they not defend their fellow Germans who happened to be Jewish? In all probability, they would say, "We were afraid of the Gestapo. They were ruthlessly cruel and would have accused us of disloyalty to Hitler and even treason.[26]

In the USA, which many consider the bastion of democracy, a disturbing number of people do not exercise their right to vote, even though they are qualified to do so. A reason given for their apparent apathy is that they do not trust politicians and believe that they are self-serving and corrupt. Be that as it may, by failing to vote, they are actually allowing themselves to be ruled by the very persons they seem to despise or mistrust.

Indecision can be brought about by a number of subtle aspects of our lives. Let us examine some of them, briefly. Our modern life is compartmentalized in various ways, ranging from church and state to fire fighting and law enforcement. We assume that decisions in one compartment of our lives do not affect other compartments, and this effectively lets us off the hook. Reality suggests that life cannot be that easily and discretely packaged: aspects of life are intertwined. They are intimately connected, related and complex. Some examples might help here.

When the twin Towers were destroyed by two jet airliners, several branches or division of rescue workers were called in to help people. Coordination of these crews was hampered by the fact that they could not communicate effectively with each other. Municipal authorities were aware of this problem but postponed decisions relating to it. In a sadly dramatic way compartmentalization prevented cooperation. The failure to equip and coordinate these rescue teams did not exempt the authorities from partial responsibility. In retrospect, they felt guilty about the loss of life caused by a lack of communication and they vowed and declared that this would not happen again. Have we really learned anything? Maybe, but we have a long way to go.[27]

Joe wanted to be successful at his job and bring home a large pay check,   so agreed to work overtime whenever he could.

Gradually, the amount of overtime increased to the point that Joe was neglecting his wife and family. When Joe complained that the amount of overtime he was doing was now excessive, the boss dismissed his complaint with "that is the price of promotion and success." Joe's wife resented her husbands continual absence from the home and felt that he cared more about his job than he did his family. The children were constantly disappointed by their father's absence from their activities and voiced their disappointment and frustration with him as well. Joe felt increasingly unappreciated and angry because he felt that his responsibility only applied to his job and nothing more. He was the breadwinner of the family.

Responsibility in one area of our lives (work) does not exempt us from responsibility for others (wife and family) even though we think it should. All is not lost if we are prepared to reorder our priorities and renegotiate our commitments. It is tough to stand up for our principles or values, but our reluctance at critical moments in our lives can be serious and cause much suffering for us and others. Letting the situation slide is a recipe for much heartache.

Peer pressure is another powerful motivator in our society. Most parents discover that when their children go to school, family values are suddenly challenged by peer pressure. Where peer pressure is operating, decisions are made mostly according to what peers think and are doing, not what parents think. The suppression of the self, in favor of the group, is an all too common reality. Family and personal values are relatively easily silenced in favor of conformity to other's wishes. Here is another example.

The dangers of smoking tobacco are well known in our society. One might think that youths would shy away from smoking in the light of documented evidence about its harmful effects, but many teenagers take up smoking. Why do they decide to do this? Peer pressure is so powerful that it can often override the fear of death, scientific evidence, common sense, parental values and their own beliefs. Teenagers find it easier to go along with peer pressure than to take a stand. Conformity can be used to persuade us to act, with devastating effects.

Another powerful but subtle influence in our lives is advertising and public relations. The ability to "engineer consent" as Edward Bernays puts it, actually undermines our ability to make decisions, though pundits of advertising and public relations would rush to deny this. Our fascination with  fashion, trend and innovation, and our desire to conform with them, is exploited by advertising. Dissatisfaction with what we already have is cultivated by advertising and provides another  strong motivation to consume new and better consumer goods. The desire to possess or own new technology conveys a sense of power and self-worth to us, that is highly seductive.  In these and other ways, we are manipulated by advertising media to make decisions to purchase goods that in many cases we really do not need.[28]

It is not only a matter of consumption and image building, it is a matter of conforming to "cultural values" that are imbedded in commercials. When people buy products they buy far more than the products themselves, they buy ideas of beauty, success, popularity, sexuality and power.  Some depth psychologists claim that individuals can be manipulated through their subconscious desires to make choices that they would not normally make. Though subliminal advertising has been discounted by most modern scholars, the very concept is fascinating and frightening,  because it appears to undermine our fundamental belief that we are free to choose.

In politics, "silent consent" is achieved when free expression and objectivity are repressed.  People feel afraid of expressing  their views, especially if they are critical of the oppressive regime. They know that their statements will result in punitive measures.  In such regimes, voices of the opposition are systematically repressed, parties are outlawed, organizations dismantled, and media are shut down.  Gradually, the voices of opposition diminish in number and strength until there is silence. This slow and systematic suppression has been called the "spiral of silence" by Elizabeth Noelle-Neumann.[29]

Though we may feel disillusioned that freedom of expression and democracy can be crushed so easily, this negative result is not the final outcome. The repressed opposition can and does work secretly, underground. In the cat and mouse campaigns which follow, timing and strategy is everything. It is vital to know when to speak and when to remain silent, when to act and when not to act. Secret organizations have tremendous power, which if well organized, can undermine even the most powerful government.

As a South African, I can testify to the truth of the above statements. Growing up during the "apartheid" era, I witnessed the systematic suppression of political movements and media. In most cases Africans were treated paternalistically as children incapable of making decisions, or even exercising their right to vote.

Numerous attempts were made to suppress black political organizations, infiltrate meetings, shut down newspapers, arrest leaders and torture detainees. The blacks were seen as the enemies of the white-dominated and controlled state; their efforts to be free were often treated as treasonous acts; their fighters, as communistically inspired terrorists.

The elaborate and idealistic system of social engineering (apartheid) worked, only through rigorous discrimination and law enforcement. Nevertheless, the hopes and aspirations of the blacks could not be muzzled. In fact, the more ruthless the white oppression became, the stronger was their desire to overcome it. Many of the resistence movements simply went underground and organized secretly. Not all the wealth of the nation, its national armies or secret police could destroy the spirit of freedom.

When Nelson Mandela was released from Robin Island, all the whites predicted that it signaled the end of South Africa, but instead, Mandela managed to establish a process of cooperation between blacks and whites.[30] It was not easy to forgive and forget, and the nation went through the agonizing process of "Truth and Reconciliation" hearings. It has been a long and painful readjustment, but the government has moved closer to embracing democratic principles, where all the people have a right to express their voice and choose their own leaders.[31]

A people cannot make intelligent and mature decisions unless it has the freedom to make decisions and learn from its mistakes. This is not an easy process, but it is the *only way* that

34

leaders will take responsibility for their destiny and be held accountable for their decisions.[32]

# PREPARATION FOR DECISION MAKING

The following preparatory conditions need to be identified before meaningful decisions can be made. Readers are invited to ask themselves the following questions:

- *Are you free to make a decision?*
- *Do you have the power or status to choose?*
- *Have you explored the options open to you?*
- *What are the advantages or disadvantages of your choice? How will you benefit from it?*
- *What are possible consequences of your choice? What will happen if you make the choice you do?*
- *Do you believe that you will be satisfied with the choice that you have made? What degree of satisfaction will you settle for?*
- *When must the decision be made? How much time do you have?*
- *What are the circumstances surrounding the decision? How much pressure is being put on you?*

Let us examine each of these questions one at a time for the sake of clarity and understanding.

- *Are you free to make a decision?*

The reader may think this is a foolish question, but if you do not have real freedom, your decision can only be made mentally or theoretically. Many spend much time and energy making a decision only to find that their decision cannot be implemented. For example, a man, who decides to build a garage before consulting town map or surveyor, may discover that the garage he is planning to build is located on a municipal easement. All the planning in the world may be for naught if he is not permitted to build there.

36

- *Do you have the power or status to choose?*

Even in a democratic political system, which holds human rights to be sacred, many people do not have the power or status to decide. For example, in certain states, contracts are dependent on the male spouse's signature. A woman might choose to buy a car, but may find that she cannot do so without her husband's signature, even if he is totally in agreement with the purchase and respects her rights. This decadent legislation raises the ire of many women who consider themselves liberated. Unfortunately, the law has not caught up with modern thinking, despite our protestations!

- *Have you explored the options open to you?*

As mentioned above, it is hard to know all the possible options you may have, but knowing *some* of the parameters may be helpful. Try to limit the number of choices to a minimum. For example, if you are a student in college, you may struggle to choose your courses for next semester. There are literally thousands of options in the college catalog, but most departments in a college have core requirements, major and minor course requirements, and even course sequences, which you must follow. An awareness of these parameters limits the number of choices you can make considerably. Sometimes, a "check sheet" will keep you on track and give you some security in the process. You are less likely to register for a course you will be barred from taking because of some missing prerequisite.

- *What are the advantages or disadvantages of your choice? How will you benefit from it?*

Connecting the dots beforehand may make some decisions easier. Remember, decisions are like the ripples in a pond. They expand ever outwards towards the bank. Your decision may not only affect you, it may affect others in your family, job, peer group, pets, environment, etc. For example, in a pet store, families often try to decide what fish to have in their aquarium. The fish all look so beautiful and attractive, but knowing some fish are aggressive and prey upon smaller ones (a decided disadvantage) may prevent

37

you from purchasing the wrong fish. On the other hand, if you know the fish are passive, "community" ones (an advantage), you can quite safely add them to your tank.

- *What are possible consequences of your choice? What will happen if you make the choice you do?*

The theoretical exploration of consequences may not always work too well for us. You cannot possibly explore all the consequences of a choice, and it is possible to underestimate, or overestimate, consequences in our mind. What we need is a touch of reality, some practical experience. Sometimes checking it out with someone a little less close to the situation, will provide confirmation. For example, at a swimming pool, children are not allowed to swim in the deep end. A mother is sure that her kids can swim well enough to enter the deep end, but she is not sure whether the lifeguard will allow them to do so. Rather than embarrass her children she discusses her predicament with one of the parents at the edge of the pool, but she shrugs her shoulders. To make sure she approaches the lifeguard directly and he shakes his head. Parents often warn children about dangerous situations and keeping rules, but they don't listen. Sometimes, getting them to imagine the consequences helps, but it may take being "balled out" by a life guard before they really pay attention to their Mom. It may takes a near drowning incident to really understand the consequences. Those who have gone through the experience like this, know whether the danger is real or not and why the rules are there!

- *Will you be satisfied with the choice that you have made? What degree of satisfaction will you settle for?*

Choosing something is one thing, being satisfied with it later, is another. In the flush of the moment, we may be satisfied, but as time wears on, we may grow more and more dissatisfied with what we chose. The idea of trying something out before you purchase it is a good one, but that is not always possible. If you have had an opportunity to experience what you chose, are you still satisfied? Partly? Mostly? Completely? Commitment quite often means living with your choice and enjoying it or cherishing it afterwards.  This is not an easy thing to do in a materialistic world that continually creates dissatisfaction in us  for old or used things.

For example, the choice of furniture for a living room may look fine in the showroom, but when is it is moved into the actual living room, it may be apparent that the carpet pattern does not go well with the upholstery of the chairs.   If you are lucky, you can return the furniture to the store, but will probably have to pay the price of restocking or transportation.  There may be other alternatives, however.  A new carpet might solve the problem, perhaps repainting the walls will do the trick, but clearly some form of compromise will have to be made.  Can you live with the compromise?   Making a choice work requires some form of accommodation or adaptation on your part.

- *When must the decision be made?  How much time do you have?*

Some decisions require immediate attention, but others have a deadline or decision date built into them.  Immediate decisions are unfortunate, but they have to be made.  A deadline is a deadline, and must be respected if you are professional, but make sure that the situation is that urgent before you panic.  A delay can be negotiated.  Some unethical sales persons deliberately give the impression that a purchasing decision must be made immediately.   If possible, always try to delay such decisions.  Try to schedule enough time to do whatever preparation is required, before making up your mind.  For example, a man is purchasing a house.  The realtor tells him that there are several interested buyers waiting to bid for the house, in a very competitive market.  When the man hesitates to close the deal, and asks for time to consult with some friends, the realtor tells him he cannot hold the sale.  To know whether the pressure is fabricated or real is critical information.  If it is real, then you do indeed have to decide, but if not. you can wait before you do.

- *What are the circumstance surrounding the decision? How much pressure is being put on you?*

Sometimes the circumstances or context within which you make a decision is critical, sometimes it is not. It is important to determine what the circumstances are and what difference they make to your decision. I knew a graduate student at SMU, who discovered that his wife was pregnant for the third time! The residence in which they were staying had a rule that couples could only stay there if they had two children, but not three. There was no doubt that they wanted the baby, but they had to move off campus, and he had to get a job. In this case the university department was incredibly helpful, arranging interviews with potential employers and finding alternative accommodation.

# APPROACHES TO DECISION MAKING

As mentioned previously, there are several "approaches" to decision making, some more relevant than others. Readers may find some approaches work better than others to meet their particular needs. A "balanced" or "holistic" decision usually involves more than one approach because life has many dimensions.

The following questions aren't in any order and may not all be relevant. Readers may choose the questions that apply to them, in whatever order they may think best. Please note that in rare instances the answers to a particular set of questions may conflict with others. An example may help to clarify the last statement.

In South Africa, many blacks have very large families. Their children often suffer from malnutrition because there are many mouths to feed and some mothers are pregnant while they are still nursing their previous child. To a westerner, it may be reasonable or logical for parents to practice birth control, so that their meager resources go further. However, effective birth control depends on carefully controlled medication or the use of condoms, neither of which methods are favored by tribal mores. Children are considered a source of wealth, not a liability. Even in western society, some Catholics regard contraception as unethical. For these reasons, cultural and spiritual questions may supercede those of reason and actually overrule them.

Consider the following questions in any combination or order:

- *What is the reasonable or logical thing to do?*
- *How do you feel about it?*
- *What does collective experience (peer group and society in general) suggest?*
- *What do family members think you should do?*
- *What do cultural values suggest?*

- *What do spiritual values suggest?*
- *What do ethical values suggest?*
- *What are possible benefits for all involved?*

In the pages that follow, you will find Check Sheets that relate to each of the questions mentioned above. Spend some time over the check sheets and write out your answers to the questions. You may find that writing clarifies your thinking. If necessary, take the questions and notes into an interview or discussion, so that you can refer to them and they can jog your memory. Discussions often wander aimlessly or get bogged down in minute details. The questions and answers may serve as a kind of agenda and keep you on track. Most people will offer their help if they see that you have done some "homework" and need help trying to sort out priorities.

As chair of a Personnel Committee of a university department, I was often involved with interviewing applicants for a position. After each interview the committee would ask the applicant if he/she had any questions. Those who had done their homework (researched our department, curriculum and structure) and who asked several relevant questions about the university, always did better than those who did not.

# RATIONAL CHECK SHEET

The assumption that most people are rational seems to be a given in this approach, however, rationality should not be taken for granted. Many people do not think or argue rationally.

It is commonly assumed that education and reason are synonymous, but I have found that sometimes even well educated people struggle with systematic or rational analysis. Objectivity is never easy. In addition, it is perfectly natural to resist anything that threatens our preconceived ideas! Also, it is not inappropriate to acknowledge our personal biases.

The maxim, "think outside the box," is a tough assignment for some, especially when their thinking is prescribed by such things as job descriptions, standard of learning exams, study guides and multiple-choice tests. In some peer groups a questioning mind is discouraged. It is regarded as a sign of "nerdism," liberalism or uncertainty, and dismissed as weakness. In my opinion, just the opposite is the case. Asking questions is a sign of intelligent health and strength. Do not let peer pressure thwart your desire to find answers to your questions!

Admitting that you do not know *is never a sign of weakness, especially if you are determined to seek the truth.* I believe we will never find confidence and certainty in ourselves unless we move beyond these initial barriers and establish a good foundation for our decision making. We must be willing to ask questions and to probe so that we understand where we stand and why.

Depending on our analytical ability, we may or may not be able to find good reasons for what we are planning, but we should try at least to voice our thoughts as sincerely and honestly as we can. It helps to articulate our thinking, when we speak to someone about it. In most cases, the fewer words we use to explain our position the better. Long sentences and complicated ideas can cause us to stray in terms of grammar and logic!

Sometimes personal biases may be evident in our explanation, including a few selfish motives. It is better to acknowledge these than to pretend they do not exist. Most people can find reasons for what they want to do, but do not be surprised if there are some flaws in your logic.[33]

It is unlikely that you will resort to formal logic, but it case you do, here are some examples. In formal logic, syllogisms may be used to check the logicality of our statements. A syllogism abbreviates the argument into symbolic form (If A then B, if B then C, etc.). A symbolic representation of your argument, may be helpful, but be careful of errors in logic. The following argument, "All dogs are canines; this animal is a canine; it must be a dog," sounds logical but it has a flaw in it. Canines include hyenas, coyotes and foxes! The animal could be any one of these, not necessarily a dog! The argument, "All dogs have whiskers; this animal has whiskers; it must be a dog," is obviously fallacious. We may laugh at its ridiculous conclusion, but similar errors in our reasoning can occur without our noticing it. That is why articulating and sharing your reasoning is so helpful.[34]

Be careful of generalizations and stereotypes.[35] You may have had a bad experience with a blond woman's intellectual ability, but that does not mean that *all blonds are dumb*.[36] Your male boss may be a pervert, but not *all men are jerks!* Hopefully, talking to a trusty and alert confidant will correct some of these mistakes and prejudices.[37]

Remember, even though you have strong and sound reasons for a course of action, you may actually reject it for other reasons. People do illogical things all the time. For example, some women marry prisoners who are on death row, and people waste all of their hard earned cash in gambling casinos. We may find these actions difficult to understand, but there may be very good reasons for all of them. Consider the following example:

## EXAMPLE

A student was born and raised in Africa. He was fascinated with television and film, but none of the universities or trade schools in his native land taught Media Studies. The young man discovered that some American universities provided the curriculum that he sought and so he applied for a scholarship at one of them. To his delight he received a scholarship and moved to the U.S. on a student visa. When he was qualified, he returned home, but found very few job opportunities there. In addition, he discovered that the ideals of a free press were not respected by his native government. Much of his work was regularly censored. Frustrated, he wondered if he should return to America.

He consulted his family and friends, they rejected his plans to emigrate as unpatriotic and foolhardy. They advised him to settle down and compromise his ideals for the sake of stability and employment. Despite the advice of family and friends, he decided to return to America and seek employment there, even if it meant renouncing the citizenship of his homeland! He assumed that he was more likely to find a job in the U.S. with his qualifications and would feel less frustrated living and working in a nation that respected freedom of the press. What would you have done if you were in his predicament? Do you think his reasoning was sound?

## QUESTIONS

1.     *In a few words, why do you think the decision is reasonable or logical?*

2.     *Given the circumstances or predicament you are in, is it logical to choose this? Describe the circumstances and their ramifications for all parties involved, if you can.*

3.     *Are there any flaws in your reasoning? Ask others to help you with this.*

4.     *Are you aware of any biases or prejudices you may have? It is OK to admit them!*

5.     *What assumptions have you made?*

6.   What facts (information) do you have to support your decision? List them.

7.   Can you prioritize the facts? Are any facts stronger or weaker than others? What is the evidence?

8.   Have you polled or consulted with others about your decision? What do they say? Is their opinion reliable or objective?

9.   What kind of pressure, if any, is being put on you to make this particular decision? Who is applying pressure? Why?

10.  What is the motivation behind the pressure? If you are not sure, give yourself some time to check out possible motivations.

# FAMILY CHECK SHEET

Many family beliefs and values are passed on unwittingly to its members. They are gradually imparted from our youth not only by our parents but by other members of our extended family, and even friends of the family. Depending on how extensive our family is, this influence can be simple or complex. When we reach puberty and our teens we may begin to question and/or rebel against the values that have been imparted to us. Sometimes peer values supercede family values, and it is hard for us to know where we stand. Our turmoil or confusion over beliefs and values may be exacerbated by family dynamics.[38]

Consulting with members of our immediate family over decisions seems a natural thing to do, but may not be productive in all cases. Unfortunately there is a lot of "baggage" in some families that gets in the way. As the saying goes, "family members are too close to us," to give us objective advice. Trusting relationships are critical to the reception of advice from others, however. If you are aware of an unspoken motivation or agenda in a family member or friend, great care should be taken when receiving such advice.

Those who are "born" into a family business or farm ownership are often expected to play an active role in its continuation. Some children see this as a responsibility, others do not. Unfortunately, much guilt is laid upon those who don't. In addition, children either admire or despise the roles that their parents play in life, wishing to follow or deviate from them. If you feel that your family is influencing your choices, it is vital to be up-front about it. You will need to determine whether your decision is the right thing to do, or whether it is a response to family obligation?

As we have noted before, parents often make decisions for their children, and out of respect the children comply with them. Usually, there comes a time when children have to be their own persons, for no other reason than that is what *they personally want*. In discussing our plans with our family, our motivation should not be to seek permission so much as to determine how our decision will affect family members from the youngest to the oldest. Depending on the age of the children, sharing all the details surrounding a decision may not be helpful, but it may become essential later on when they are more mature.[39]

Children's ability to understand the full implications of a decision should not be underestimated, however, nor should their opinions and feelings be discounted. Their reasons for or against a decision may be vastly different from yours but you need to respect them.

Do not expect every member in your family to support your plans or agree with you, but you should be able to judge the consensus, if any, of the family. Consulting can be done with individual members, or as a group. Recognize and accept minority feelings or attitudes, if any, found in the group.

As mentioned above, group dynamics in some families are not healthy. If the situation becomes counter productive, abort the discussion, and try a one to one approach. Only you can be the judge of which approach is better.

Also, the timing of consultation is important. People need time to think about what you are saying, and should not be rushed or pounced upon.

One should allow for the fact that close family members may be afraid of hurting your feelings, and may therefore, avoid telling the truth. It is very hard to be objective when dealing with those close to us. Consulting with friends outside the family might provide necessary correction and balance.

Remember that you should follow a family member's advice only if you are satisfied that it is the right thing for you to do. Be careful of allowing loyalty or guilt to persuade you. You must make up your own mind.

## EXAMPLE

Tommy owned a feed mill which he had built up from scratch. He was well liked by the farmers in his community and the business soon prospered. During the holidays he invited his son, Roger, to work at the mill and payed him well for his efforts. As he worked along side his father Roger soon picked up all aspects of the business. When he went to college Tommy encouraged him to take courses in accounting and marketing, but Roger wanted to study art with a minor in photography. Tommy tried to put pressure on his boy by refusing to pay his tuition if he persisted in taking art classes. Roger refused to listen to his father and wanted to know why he was doing this. Tommy explained that art would not help him to run a feed mill. Roger replied, "What makes you think I want to run a feed mill?" Tommy was shocked by this frank reply and admitted that he assumed his son would follow in his footsteps.

## QUESTIONS

1. *Is the time and place appropriate for family members so that they can give you their undivided attention?*

2. *In what way is your family influencing your decisions?*

3. *Have you explained to your family members why you want to make certain decisions?*

4. *Have you shared why you are having a difficult time deciding?*

5. *What do you think the implications of your decision are for members of your family?*

6. *Do they concur with your perceptions and insights? If not, what are you going to do?*

7. *Do family members feel positively or negatively about what you have proposed?*

8.  Do you sense that some members are hiding their feelings because they are afraid of hurting you?

9.  How do you feel about this hidden agenda? Acknowledge the feelings you have and try to keep calm.

10. Enquire whether they have experienced what you are going through, if not exactly, then maybe partly.

11. Ask them to imagine they are in your shoes at this moment. What would they do?

12. Try to distinguish between agreement and understanding. (Family members may understand you without necessarily agreeing with your decision)

# EXPERIENCE CHECK SHEET

Most children roll their eyes when parents offer advice or talk about their past experience. Children usually believe that they must experience life first-hand to appreciate it, and the generation gap between them and their elders sometimes precludes any meaningful sharing.

It would be foolish to assume that the "school of hard knocks," has to be experienced before anyone learns something. We do not have to reinvent the wheel to take advantage of it, but sometimes people are reluctant to learn from history or their mistakes. *If we are to benefit from the experience of others, we must be willing to learn from both their successes and their failures. The simple awareness that someone else recognizes your predicament, and has lived through it, is comforting news!*

A common misconception is that what we are going through is unique to us and therefore no one is really capable of helping us. No one will deny the essential uniqueness of your experience, but in reality what you consider unique may not be that unique after all. Each generations' experiences are limited by time and environment, but there are always common elements, essential experiences, that transcend them and link us together. We must learn to identify these common elements and evaluate them accordingly.

Some people are convinced that their own experience is the only criterion for a decision. They tend to dismiss psychological or philosophical insights as being too theoretical. Most of the human sciences hold that theory and practice are strongly linked and necessary to each other. .

While experiences are very informative, they can be misleading especially if the outcome of the experience has been negative and the person involved has become prejudiced or biased. It is wise to ask the advice of several people with similar experiences so that you can compare and contrast them.

Today, "collective wisdom and experience" is readily available from many sources in our culture, outside of our family.

51

Sources include good friends, counselors and teachers. In addition, the Internet has become a tool of collective sharing, which some would liken to a global village. E-mail and "blogs" provide avenues for us to share deep and intimate experiences which in the past would have been unthinkable.

We must recognize that the "providers" of some experience and advice are professional, other are not. Whether we trust their wisdom or not, depends on many things, such as, their credibility, education, qualifications, congeniality, motivation, age, character and so on. Needless to say, we must be careful about the experience we derive from sources that are not familiar to us.

Because persons on the Internet and on television appear to be authoritative and persuasive does not mean that they are so in fact. Con artists are notorious for exploiting gullible people. Be on your guard when and if you become involved with them.

## EXAMPLE

A few years away from retirement, a professor decided he would like to learn to fly an ultra-light aircraft. The choice of aircraft and flight school were two important decisions he had to make. Having shopped around, he found a new Six Shooter para-wing aircraft at a reasonable price.

Of all the experimental aircraft he felt safer in it because the parachute was already deployed. Two instructors offered to teach him, one who bragged about his qualifications and spoke of his peers with contempt, and the other a humble man who had served as an aircraft mechanic in the armed services and was a qualified pilot with instructor rating.

In observing the two instructors, he noticed the meticulous care that the second instructor took of his aircraft and how cautious he was to check every system before his pupils took off. He talked to qualified pilots and asked them about their experience with the instructors. After assessing their remarks, the choice was fairly easy because of first-hand experience and the confirmation of the other pilots. Training was started, and in the process confirmed the choice. In retrospect, he was glad that he had not been hoodwinked by the arrogant instructor and that he had the common sense to consult with other pilots.

## QUESTIONS

1. *From whom are you seeking advice? List all the people and their relationship to you. Why are you approaching them?*

2. *What are their qualifications? Expertise? Experience?*

3. *Is there any way you can watch them interacting with others?*

4. *How credible are they? Honest? Reliable? Reputation?*

5. *How long have you known them?*

6. *How long have they done what you are seeking to do or experience?*

7. *How do you know they have actually done what you are about to do or experience?*

8. *Do you trust them? Why?*

9. *Have they been successful? Unsuccessful?*

10. *Can you learn from their experiences?*

11. *How does their experience relate to yours?*

# EDUCATION CHECK SHEET

There are many misconceptions about education that should be recognized. Education is often touted as the gateway to job procurement and success. *While this may be generally true, the fact is many graduates do not find jobs in their field, partly because they lack experience and partly because they are not persistent enough.* For this reason, many academic institutions now insist that students take *practica* and/or internships in their field, before they go job hunting.

A typical assumption is that educated persons make decisions more easily. Though educated people undoubtedly have access to more information, and may know how to gather and interpret it, they may not apply it wisely.

Sometimes too much information can confuse and overwhelm us, and sorting out the forest from the trees can be difficult. Nevertheless, if an educated person is well trained he or she is more likely to think more analytically and clearly.

Many people also assume that educated persons are wiser than others. Sadly, even learned professors are not necessarily experienced or wise in personal or domestic matters. Most persons with Ph.D.s are experts in a very narrow field and their research is correspondingly specialized. It should come as no surprise that they are not necessarily experts in fields outside of their speciality.

As one who has earned several highly specialized degrees, and taught in higher education for many years, I have been surprised at how some educated people are self-opinionated and biased. A few even lack social graces, common sense, and management skills! These statements should not be interpreted as a sign of disloyalty to my colleagues, or disrespect for their qualifications.

Today, most educational decisions are job related. Students and parents want to know what qualifications are necessary for a particular job. They also want to know which schools will provide the best preparation for the job.

It is highly likely there are several schools with good training and preparation, and students may need to visit several of them before making up their minds.

While these utilitarian questions are appropriate, it should be recognized that education in general is not necessarily job related. *Education is for a life time, and during that time most people will make several career changes. When students graduate what is important is not that they are trained for a particular career, but that they are equipped to make good decision, switch careers, retool and retrain. Ultimately, students need to determine whether what education will equip them to adapt and survive in an ever changing world environment.*

Information about what training is required for a job may also be a little confusing. Some professions are biased in favor of theoretical education while others are not. I will never forget over hearing a television station manager speaking contemptuously about his camera operators: "Why do you need to go to college to run a camera? Give me a bunch of monkeys and I will teach them how to do it in five minutes!" This statement is foolish as it is biased.

Needless to say, schools that offer Media Studies curricula will disagree with the derogatory comment. There is, however, an element of truth to the manager's comment. *Practical experience is vital to a person in this field.* Does this mean that all the other course work is valueless? Of course not. It is important to understand that few videographers stay in videography throughout their whole career. They move on to better and higher paid positions.

Sometimes it takes several sessions with a chosen advisor or professional to know whether their advice is balanced and helpful or not. Advisors, on the other hand, should not hesitate to refer students to faculty members who have more experience in a particular field than they do.

## EXAMPLE

A young man was interested in becoming a doctor. He applied to several medical schools and was accepted by one that he considered a last resort. In researching the background of this program, he discovered that its reputation was far from shabby, and that there was some cutting edge medical research going on there. Toward the end of his final year, he began to think about what kind of medicine he wanted to practice. There were many specialities to choose from. He chose family medicine, but a year later, he found he was less and less interested in family medicine. Some of his colleagues put a lot of pressure on him to complete what he had started, because there was a great need for family practice physicians at the time.

In one of his rotations he came across sleep medicine and he investigated this field. Several teaching hospitals provided rotations in sleep medicine, but he found that doctors in the field generally came from two "specialties," psychiatry and neurology. He found that his peers and attending doctors seemed divided over which background was appropriate for sleep medicine. Unfortunately, many of the neurologists were contemptuous of candidates from any other fields. Clearly, he would have to choose one or the other of them, but the arrogance and contemptuousness of the doctors disturbed him, and ultimately, he chose psychiatry.

## QUESTIONS

1.  *Do you know what education you need to accomplish the career goals you have in mind?*

2.  *Does the curriculum and learning environment provided by the school/s relate to practical and real life situations?*

3.  *Have you interviewed professionals in the fields to which you aspire? How do they suggest you prepare for your career?*

4.  *Do you know which professors will teach you? Are their qualifications and/or experience relevant?*

5. *Have you discussed the credentials and reputation of the professors with graduates, peers and students?*

6. *Have you visited the university environments in which you will learn (classrooms, labs, etc.)?*

7. *Are there any signs of prejudice in their approach to teaching? How open are "the experts" to questions, new ideas, innovation and technology?*

8. *Are the teachers humble enough to admit their limitations and refer you to other qualified people?*

9. *Are you paying attention to your "common sense" or "gut feelings" about the learning environment?*

# CULTURE CHECK SHEET

American culture is often described as a "melting pot" because its origins may be found in many cultures. Though most of its citizens are proud of their cultural heritage they are equally proud of being an American. The mixture or blending of cultures into a unified whole with one language and one constitution is an amazing achievement. Most Americans believe that their nation is enriched, not impoverished, by the influence of these cultural elements upon each other, like the ingredients in a tasty bowl of soup.[40]

In the past it was expected that immigrants would break free from their cultural roots and ethnic origins, learn English and accept a new national identity. This expectation has changed over the years and now many of the new immigrants are retaining their cultural ties with their homeland, and even their own language. Sociologists now refer to America as a "salad bowl," because each of the ingredients in a salad retains its individual characteristic and is not blended together. In may cases, where people settle in America determines with which ethnic group they identify.[41]

Today, when families emigrate or move from one country to another, they tend to maintain many of their cultural values and practices. The degree to which adaption to the new environment occurs depends on the strength of their connection to the "homeland." Older adults may tend to preserve more of their cultural heritage than their children. Sometimes conflict develops between newer and older generations of immigrants over how much or how little of their culture should be preserved. The gulf is usually accompanied by much pain and misunderstanding.[42]

Family members either conform or do not conform with the cultural norms with which they were raised. Over time, ties with their homeland weaken, and cultural heritages are kept or discarded. Within the new environment, families develop their own traditions and values. Many of the disagreements in families arise over issues of conformity, values, manners and discipline.[43]

How you react to the dominant culture in your environment

will influence your decisions. Concepts such as "success," "fame," "vocation" and "parenting" are commonly derived from popular literature and entertainment, but perhaps the greatest influence of all is personal encounters with family members.

In many cases, our understanding of the roles played by various professions, and our expectations of ourselves, is culturally determined. How do you judge who is a successful husband or mother or doctor or plumber or teacher? What professions are considered to be more honorable than others? What behavior in these professions is appropriate and what is not?

Individuals must determine where they stand on many of these issues.

## EXAMPLE

After the attack on Pearl Harbor, many Japanese-Americans were considered suspect, regardless of their loyalty to our nation. Some were arrested and detained in camps and their families suffered harsh discrimination. Many Americans justified these actions on the grounds that internal security must be preserved in a time of war. Nevertheless, it was a sad and hurtful mistake. The Japanese immigrants considered themselves Americans, even though many of their prejudiced contemporaries did not. [44]

After September 11th, many loyal Americans were similarly mistreated for similar reasons because of their assumed connection with Iraq. Had history repeated itself? Not exactly, but the biases and prejudices were the same, and they blinded many Americans to the past. They did not recognize the loyalty of many of their fellow citizens. How had these attitudes developed? Upon what were they based? Was the angry and bitter reaction of some mid-easterners in America justified?

Some Iraqis and Iranians are confused about their prejudicial treatment and how they should behave in the light of it. Should they be proud or embarrassed about their ethnic origins? Parents and children are divided. Unfortunately, hostility is rampant and cruel, and some "international students" have decided not to return to their universities because they fear prejudicial treatment.

## QUESTIONS

1. *To what extent are you influenced by your cultural roots? Are you proud of them? Embarrassed by them?*

2. *Do you feel vulnerable and sometimes defensive about your culture? Why?*

3. *Do you recognize that not all the members of your family have adapted equally well to new American culture?*

4. *Which of your personal values are derived from your family and its cultural background?*

5. *How different are your values form American values? What values do you think you should preserve? What should you discard?*

6. *What expectations of do you have of yourself and others in your family, as far as cultural values are concerned?*

7. *Are there differences between the older and younger generations of your family? What are they?*

8. *Have you recognized what powerful emotions may be attached to different values?*

9. *Have you tried to discuss the above questions objectively and calmly with your family?*

# RELIGION CHECK SHEET

The term "vocation" was once used to describe the work people did. The theology behind this term assumes that God calls individuals to follow particular careers. In addition, it is believed that God gives us different "talents" or gifts, to enabled us to accomplish various trades, crafts and professions to serve humanity and earn a living. In secular colleges and universities, today, two of the most important motivations for choosing a career are money and interest. Sometimes, students consider service as a priority, but sadly, even that is a lessor priority. Knowing where you stand in terms of your religion may be critically important to you.

Most readers will find decisions involving spiritual values most challenging, simply because God's purposes and imperatives are not easy to define or apply to human situations. In addition, such values depend on our conception of God, and what kind of relationship we have with Him or Her.

Throughout history people have sought guidance in spiritual matters from four sources: scripture, tradition, reason and experience. Depending on the religion and its organizational divisions, some of these sources are valued more highly than others. In general, the authority of holy scripture has precedence over all the other sources.

In the case of the Jewish religions, the authority stems primarily from a covenant based on the ten commandments which were given to Moses and later interpreted and applied by prophets, priests and kings. Christians believe that this covenant was renewed and completed by Jesus and his teaching has been conveyed to the Church by his Disciples and Apostles. Muslims rely heavily on the teaching and writings of Mohammed or particular Caliphs and Mullahs.

We should recognize that the experience of God's revelation throughout history is not consistently the same, nor conventional by any means. A comparison of the calling of a number of great prophets in holy scripture will demonstrate this fact. God spoke to

Moses through a *burning bush* out in the desert. Elijah heard God's voice in *a quiet whisper* at the entrance of a cave. Isaiah had a vision of God *in a smoke filled temple,* where his lips were symbolically purged with a hot coal from the altar. Paul saw *a bright light* on the road to Damascus where he was going to arrest and persecute Christians. [45]

Because these revelations are so different, and we ourselves are unique individuals, we should not necessarily expect God to use similar means to reveal Himself to us. Nor should we be upset if some in the religious community express cautious scepticism about our experience. For example, the people of Israel questioned Moses about his leadership several times. Jesus was constantly challenged by religious leaders of his time, and finally put to death by them for blasphemy. In almost every place Paul went on his missionary journeys he was thwarted by Jews who questioned his theology.

Most believers are moved by the examples of key figures in their holy scriptures or ecclesiastical history. Their life and ministry is compelling because they admire their insights and examples. However, modern believers can only follow these examples to a certain degree. Differences in time, place, culture, life-style and temperament, demand some form of adaptation to present day life and circumstances.

Understanding our faith community's world-view is also very important. Some faiths consider the world to be so corrupt it is worthless. Salvation for them can only be achieved by withdrawing from the world, and preparing for a life in Heaven. Others believe that though the world is corrupt, it has been redeemed by God, who rescues the fallen, and helps humanity survive in it.

To avoid disappointment and frustration, it is critically important to authenticate your experiences within your faith-community. You should not make any spiritual decisions until you have checked out your conclusions with good people that you can trust within that community. Quakers refer to this body of believers as a "clearness committee." It is their purpose to help you clarify your thinking and evaluate your sense of calling. [46]

## EXAMPLE

Robert was a multi-talented youth with many interests and a good academic record. Raised in a religious home, he believed that God had a purpose for his life, and that he should serve Him in some way. The problem was, he did not know what kind of service was appropriate. His Christian faith allowed for several kinds of ministry, including pastoral work, medicine, education, and so on.

His father did not help much because he believed that, though a person could serve God as a minister, he could serve God equally well in other ways. He believed that by identifying what talents or gifts he had, he could use these gifts to please God.

In college, Robert become interested in sociology and wondered if he should become a social worker. He investigated various kinds of positions in the Peace Corp and applied for them.

After serving in the Peace Corp, he developed a keen interest in flying! Most of is friends could not understand the connection between flying and social service, but they felt sure he would sort this out eventually. His new found interest seemed such a radical switch from his earlier career plans.

To everybody's consternation and amazement, he decided to enlist in the army and began training as a helicopter pilot. To Robert, his military service was really a means to an end. He could not afford the cost of flying lessons, nor accumulate the number of hours required, as a civilian. He reasoned that he could combine his interest in flying with a being a Medivac helicopter pilot. In this way, he could serve God and society as well as do what he loved.. This decision however had a risk associated with it. He might have to go to war.

## QUESTIONS

*1.     Do you believe that God has a purpose for your life?*

2.   How has God called you to serve Him? Directly? Indirectly? How do you know this?

3.   Do you have a religious role model? Do you feel you must follow his/her example? How?

3.   Have you consulted with trustworthy individuals, in your faith community, to see if they come to the same conclusion that you do about your calling?

4.   Do you know specifically what God is calling you to do? How sure are you?

5.   Do you believe God has given you specific gifts or talents to use? What are they?

6.   Where do you think God wants you to work?

7.   Has you faith community recognized your gifts?

8.   What existing ministries are open to you? Can you work within them?

9.   Is your particular calling different from existing types of ministry? How different?

10.  Have you measured your decisions with the criteria of scripture, tradition, reason and experience?

11.  Have you shared your views with members of your family? How have they reacted?

# ETHICAL CHECK SHEET

Many modern people dismiss ethical ideals by categorizing them as religious. Since they believe in the separation of church and state, ethics are effectively disconnected from secular society and not applicable to it. Nevertheless, much of American culture and civilization is influenced by sacred and secular ethics. Even if we reject the religious roots of the Constitution, as some atheists do, they still believe in human rights and will defend them with their lives. [47]

In addition to these influences, many of our ethical ideals are derived from secular philosophers such as Aristotle, Kant, Mills and others. For example, many believe in a golden mean of moderation, a middle ground between two extremes. This principle has its origin in Aristotelian philosophy. Some also believe in embracing principles which will benefit a majority of people, a ideal promoted by Mills. If we believe in applying rules which are universally applicable to all people, we are aligning ourselves with Kantian philosophy. [48]

In the absence of secular and sacred ethics many modern people have adopted hedonistic principles. Hedonists may not be bothered much with the ethics of decision making, because they are motivated by the pleasure principle of instant gratification. For this reason, the ideas of delayed gratification, through discipline and self-sacrifice are typically unpopular and rejected by many of them.

Most elderly people react negatively to a hedonistic philosophy or lifestyle, because it seems selfish and irresponsible. Though our society encourages freedom of expression, it does not exempt people from accountability. Freedoms are seldom achieved without discipline and self-sacrifice, if not on our part, then on the part of others.

Nevertheless, we are strangely fascinated by "lawless pleasure seekers," like Bonny and Clyde or Jesse James. Living recklessly without constraint is somehow admirable to some, even though they may deny it. Secretly we envy anyone who can do whatever they like. Evidence of this can be found in "groupies" who hang around infamous criminals and murderers and who are so much in awe of them that they will obey their trivial wishes or commands (for example, Charles Manson and his followers).

Regardless of the source of our ethical ideals and how pure they may be, ethics must be applied to real life, or they will lose their meaning and relevance. Unfortunately, it is in the application of ethics that many of the problems lie.

Typically three questions are asked: In what situation are the ethics applied (situational ethics)? For example, a doctor would not pull the plug of a patient that had reasonable hope of recovery, but might do so if the patient was brain dead, with no hope of recovery.

To what other ethics can they be compared (relative ethics)? For example a Zulu woman may walk around her village bare breasted without question, but an American woman would be arrested if she did so in her neighborhood!

In what ways will it benefit us (ethics of expediency)? For example, it might be considered expedient for the United States to invade Iraq and establish democracy there, if that would secure access to the rich oil fields. Expediency should not be confused with ethical correctness.

Ethics of expediency are determined to a large degree by self-interest and many consider it to be unworthy of consideration. Nevertheless they are commonly used in modern political decisions.

In conclusion, as you approach the ethical dimensions of your decisions, it may be helpful to recognize what the source or origin of the ethical ideals are, how they relate to each situation, and what benefit you will derive from them.


## EXAMPLE

A school boy was going home one day when and came across a packet lying on the side of the road. He was going to leave it there but his curiosity caused him to turn back and see what was in it. To has amazement it contained a stack of new $100.00 bills. At first he was not going to show it to his mother, but when he did, she told him to take it to the police station near their home. She believed that keeping the money was on a par with stealing because he had not earned it. On the way to the police he met up with some of his pals who told him he was crazy to hand it over to them and he should keep the money for himself. He decided to take his pal's advice and said nothing to the police or his mother. When his mother checked with the police, the next day, she asked them what they thought about her son's find. The police did not know what she was talking about and she discovered to her dismay that he had not followed her advice. His mother insisted that he do as he was told. This time he complied with her wishes even though he did not appreciate her motivation and his friends thought he was stupid.

## QUESTIONS

1.  *Do you recognize some form of ethical principles to be binding upon your life? What are they?*

2.  *Do you adhere to the ethical principles or teachings of the founder of your faith?*

3.  *Have you considered how the teachings (examples or roles) of these leaders affect or influence your life?*

4.  *Have you tried to apply these ethical ideals to your specific predicament, or situation?*

5.  *What do you believe is the ethical or right thing to do? Do you believe it is honest, truthful, respectful, and just?*

6.  *Will what you decide benefit the maximum number of people? Is this important to you?*

7.      *Would you like what you do to become a universal law, that is, become applicable to all human beings on the face of the earth?*

8.      *Would you like to be treated by others in the same way that you treat them?*

9.      *Do you consider human life to be sacred and supremely valuable? How does this affect your choices?*

10.     *Do you think the situation or circumstance should determine the way you act?*

11.     *Given you situation, are you aware that not everyone will choose the way you do?*

12.     *Are your choices motivated by self-interest? Is this acceptable to you?*

# EMOTIONAL CHECK SHEET

Emotional responses are perfectly natural and should not be discounted or suppressed. Sometimes people refer to "emotional baggage" as if emotions are a liability or disadvantage. On the contrary, emotions are an wonderful part of our personality. [49]

Human beings have an amazing range of emotional expression, usually associated with people, confrontation, circumstances, persuasion and sexuality. The outpouring of emotion can be used to measure how deeply we are involved.

The ability to control emotion and use it to one's advantage can be a powerful skill. Such skill is not confined to adult strategy, however, children at an early age are masters of manipulation! At what point does emotional expression become negative? We typically consider self-centered emotions associated with strong desires to be negative and unselfish ones to be positive. For example, compare the emotions of greed and pride with those of generosity and gratitude. [50]

If allowed to dominate to the exclusion of all else, emotions can be very dangerous, especially if they lead to impulsive or hasty decisions. Most quick and emotional decisions are regretted afterwards. In the heat of the moment, people can say and do incredibly foolish things, but in retrospect, when they have calmed down, they usually reprimand themselves for being irresponsible. It is clear that emotional decisions are not wrong in themselves, but need to be checked or balanced by other criteria.

When confronted with an emotionally loaded decision, if possible, ask for more time to consider your options. Anyone who puts pressure on you to make hasty decisions should be suspect.

More positively, it is quite appropriate to feel strongly when we decide to do something. What we feel is very important and we should not deny it. Emotions are a powerful side of life and add depth and meaning to it. Strong feelings are often associated with major changes or losses, for example, when we put a dog down, or sell an old house, or go through a divorce, or put an elderly parent in a retirement community.

In some cultures, emotion is regarded as a weakness and stereo-typically attributed to women. In such cultures it is appropriate for a women to cry, but men must maintain a "stiff upper lip"in all circumstances. Regardless of our gender, suppressed emotions have a nasty habit of escaping our control when we least expect them to. For this reason, it is not wise to stifle them. Rather we should express them spontaneously and naturally and not be embarrassed by them.

Aristotle believed that persuasion was most powerful when an emotional appeal was included in the mix, and this strategy is apparent in many modern commercials. Since emotion is regarded as a powerful tool of those who are in the business of persuasion, perhaps we should give it more attention than we do. Let us note that in commercials we are subjected to emotive pressure, as an overture to decision making that leads to consumption.

Sometimes people fail to express their opinions, because they are afraid of hurting feelings. So they use innuendos, or suggestions, or generally "beat around the bush," in their attempt to tell the truth. Of course this "sensitivity" to a person's feelings may border on lying, but we justify it as necessary anyway.

Most counselors believe it is better to recognize and express our emotions than to pretend that they are not there. Giving others permission to tell the truth, even though it hurts our feelings, can avoid "tactful dishonesty" in the feedback process. Unfortunately, not many are strong enough to brave the emotional impact of honesty. The ability to control emotional reactions can be a strength, but too much control may result in apparent "coldness" or "insensitivity." The balance of reason and emotion is an ideal goal and we should strive after it. This is the goal of Aristotelean philosophy!

## EXAMPLE

Elizabeth had two children at an early age. Whenever she

went to the store, her children seemed to misbehave; running, shouting and fighting. They would constantly nag her for items she was unwilling to buy. No matter how hard she tried, she seemed unable to control them in public. She overheard shop attendants whispering about her and some of the "well-meaning" patrons suggested various ways to discipline her children.

One day, after a long session of nagging in the same store, she decided to do something about their behavior. She pulled down their pants and spanked them hard, in front of the horrified and critical patrons.

Elizabeth was so embarrassed, she stormed out of the store, leaving her groceries behind. In her car, she broke down and sobbed. She felt humiliated and guilty, regretting that she had lost control. Perhaps most hurtful of all was her feeling that she was being judged a bad mother by some of the people.

Her reaction was perfectly natural, and most parents can identify with what happened, spanking and all! The problem was she reacted in the heat of the moment and regretted her loss of control. It is easy to offer alternative strategies, but sometimes babysitters are not available or affordable at such times. Emotion can accumulate to the point of exhaustion or anger which leads to regrettable decisions. We need to understand this.

## QUESTIONS

1.  *How strongly do you feel about the decision you are about to make?*

2.  *Is there conflict between what you feel and what you believe is rational or right?*

3.  *At this moment, which is stronger, reason or emotion?*

4.  *Are your feelings interacting with each other. Are they mixed (e.g. fear, hurt and anger all in one)?*

5. *Are stereotypes or generalizations affecting how you feel? (e.g. your future spouse is a cop or doctor)*

6. *Do you feel judged by any person because of your emotional reactions? Who?*

7. *How do others feel about your decision? Are they being honest?*

8. *In retrospect, how do you feel about what you decided?*

9. *If you were flustered or angry, have you had time to cool down and calm yourself? Do you still feel the way you did before?*

# CONSEQUENCES
# CHECK SHEET

It may be trite to say that we live in a cause and effect world. On a simple level we know this almost instinctively, but there is a big difference between thinking about consequences or outcomes and actually taking steps to implement them. Having good intentions is not the same as doing something about them.

Sometimes we pretend that we did not know what the consequences were when we landed up in trouble. This "deliberate amnesia" is a major problem in our society. Some people are not willing willing to own up to the consequences of their actions and in a few instances it may be true that we do not know why we acted the way we did or what the outcome would be.

In the natural sciences, cause and effect is easier to measure or quantify, but in the human sciences, the consequences are much more complicated and involved. This knowledge should not prevent us from trying to identify possible consequences![51]

Predicting what the consequences of a decision will be is very difficult and there is a real danger that we overestimate or underestimate the outcomes. For this reason, it is important to come up with some measure of probability, rather than making wild guesses. As we all know, human imagination is very fertile and feeds upon itself, quite often leading to exaggeration and even panic reactions. For this reason, *we should seek evidence that what we decide will in fact affect people, or situations, in the way we anticipate.* [52]

Once a process is set in motion, it may be difficult to stop or reverse. Knowing whether it is reversible or not can reduce the amount of pressure that we experience when we contemplate our actions. It is also important to know whether the decision will have short term or long term effects. We tend to be less concerned about short term effects than long term effects.

Sometimes consequences and side effects are not predictable

and may startle us. Assessing whether we are comfortable or not with the outcome may be critical at this point. The longer we are reminded of the consequences of our actions, the harder it is to deal with. Some people have a delight in rubbing salt into a wound, if they believe your decision was wrong and they are suffering as a result!

Knowing who will suffer, rather than what will happen, is probably more important. Somehow we are more sensitive to the "fallout" if the "victims" are innocent, or defenseless, for example, children or elderly parents. Even if people are aware of the risks they are taking, they need to be warned in advance so they can be prepared, and certainly not be caught off-guard.

It may be appropriate to protected someone from the consequences of a decision. It may be that children are too young to understand the ramifications, or you are afraid that they will be overwhelmed with the complexity of the situation. Make sure that your motives are pure and clear as these secondary decisions may backfire.

## EXAMPLE

Eric and Jesse decided after a number of tumultuous years to get a divorce. They discussed the implications of their divorce with attorneys and counselors and seemed fairly satisfied with the resulting division of their personal belongings. It was agreed that Jesse would look after the children but that they would have joint custody. Eric and Jesse began to pack in preparation for the move, but they did not explain what was happening to their three children. Whenever the children asked why their parents were doing what they were, they found some excuse to cover their behavior. Eventually, it became harder and harder for Jesse to explain why their father was not living with them. At last, the children demanded to know what was going on. Understandably, they were very angry that they had not been told earlier. It took them a number of weeks to work through feelings of betrayal, as well as accepting the finality of their parents' decision. Though hard to do at the time, explaining the consequences of our actions may help everyone adapt more easily in the long run. Of course it depends on how old the children are, but the older they are the more explanation they will need and expect.

Sadly, many couples only see decisions like this in the light of their own personal sacrifices or pain, and not in terms of others involved, usually their children.

## QUESTIONS

1.  *Have you explored the consequences of your decision?*

2.  *Describe the consequences as you see them.*

3.  *Are the consequences imagined or realistic?*

4.  *Are there short term consequences? Long term?*

5.  *Can you live with the consequences?*

6.  *Who specifically will be affected by your decision?*

7.  *Have you shared the consequences with them?*

8.  *How will they be affected? Can you say?*

9.  *How have family members reacted? Positively? Negatively?*

10. *Have any of these assessments changed your mind?*

# GOAL-SETTING
# CHECK SHEET

If the concept of "goal-setting" seems a little intimidating, it should not be. Perhaps a more simple way of describing goal-setting is "identifying hopes" or "articulating dreams," but it is important to retain some realism. Are the hopes and dreams achievable in a specific time frame? Unfortunately, the goals in life that we strive after are often set by others, not ourselves. Accepting the goals which others set for us can be a major problem and we need to distinguish between the two.

Regardless of their origin, there are a number of important considerations that need to be recognized in goal setting.[53] Goals need to be simple. If they are too complicated, they are harder to reach.

They need to be at an appropriate level, neither too high nor too low. If they are too low, they will be reached with little effort and there is no challenge in that. If they are too high, they cannot be reached without incredible effort and that can be discouraging. In addition, the goals that are set should be limited in terms of number and duration. Too many goals will be hard to accomplish and, if spread over a long period of time, they will become boring or tedious.

What is at stake here is our self-worth and satisfaction. Self-worth is enhanced by reaching worthy goals and a great deal of satisfaction is derived from doing so, especially if the goals are few in number and accomplished within a short time. It is for this reason that Alcoholics Anonymous recommends that recovering alcoholics "live one day at a time."

It is also helpful to set realizable steps in reaching goals so that progress can be measured incrementally. Each step reached becomes a sign of success and a moment for congratulation. Rewards are important, but should not be overdone.

Working with "coaches" or "fellow pilgrims" is also

recommended, not only because they keep us accountable but because they share in the joy of achievement. Articulating goals is essential, so that others can share in your plans, rather than being kept in the dark.

Failure to reach goals should not become a feeding frenzy of self-recrimination or blame. Failure is a common part of every person's life. Acknowledging failure, or rather, admitting that goals have not been met, is quite appropriate, provided it leads to reassessment, regrouping and starting again.

## EXAMPLE

Lucy and Harold were reaching the age of retirement. Though their employers provided good retirement packages, they both felt that they should save more by deducting greater amounts off their salaries each month. Since the additional amounts were not big, they felt that they could manage them. As time went on, they found it harder and harder to keep up with their monthly debts. They became discouraged and apprehensive. Their children were struggling to establish themselves at the time and asked for financial help on occasion. Lucy and Harold felt guilty because they could not help them. They tried to explain their predicament to their children, but were not sure they understood. By providing for their retirement, they felt they would be less dependent on their children in later life. It was hard for them to decide whether they should reduce the monthly pension deductions and have more to live on, day by day, or to leave their deductions as they were, and secure a better retirement. In talking to their children they found that they respected their parent's decision and believed that they were doing the right thing.

## QUESTIONS

1.  *What are the primary goals of your life at present? At the moment, restrict yourself to three goals, and no more.*

2.      *Are the goals realizable?  Too high?  Too low?*

3.      *What steps need to be taken to reach each goal?
        List five steps for each goal.*

4.      *Set yourself a possible time table for each goal.  How long
        will it take to reach these?  Is the time sufficient?*

5.      *Identify the first step you must take and do it.
        Take one step at a time.*

6.      *Share your goals and timetable with an objective friend or
        family member.*

7.      *If necessary reward yourself if you have achieved a step.
        Avoid going overboard with celebration!*

8.      *If you fail, do not beat up on yourself.  Reset your goal and
        try again.*

9.      *Be honest with your friend or family member, do not
        deceive yourself or others.*

# BALANCE SHEET

Before you start a balance sheet, you should try to determine whether you are an optimist or pessimist! It is important for you to determine this beforehand, because, if you have already made up your mind about the outcome, there is no need to weigh up the pros and cons!

As most people know, a balance sheet in accounting has a debit and credit side and by adding up the numbers on each side, a total is reached. If accounting is done honestly, there can be no doubt where you stand financially.

When it is hard to make up your mind about something, it is sometimes helpful to add up the pros and cons as you would a balance sheet. This exercise can be done mentally, but it is better to write the items down in two parallel columns on a piece of paper.

If you have more pros than cons, then probably the decision will be a positive one. If you have more cons than pros, it is likely your decision will be a negative one. There are two problems with this method, which should be mentioned; one is the columns end up being equal, which leaves you in the same quandary you were in before you started, and two, some of the items may be more important than others.

To determine the importance of items, they can be prioritized by means of weighting, with the most important being given the highest number, and the least important, the lowest number. Now, the highest score on one side or the other should give you some indication of the direction you should go.

Additional columns can be added which will reflect weights for emotions, consequences, short term effects, long term effects, etc., but the more complex the method becomes, the harder it is to interpret the results!

## EXAMPLE

John fell in love with a shy young woman named Mary, but she was hesitant to marry him. He was not sure what to do, since he was reluctant to put pressure on her to make up her mind. Coincidently, John was offered an engineering job in a foreign country. The job offer increased the complexity of his decision and he felt torn between the two. The job was a fabulous opportunity in terms of pay, experience and promotion but, if he went away, he might lose the love of his life, and that he could not bear. He was not sure the risk was worth it. Perhaps knowing that he was going away would precipitate her decision, in which case both opportunities might present themselves; marriage and promotion. John took the job and left the country. After two weeks of separation, Mary agreed to marry John. She flew out to be with him and the knot was tied.

## QUESTIONS

1.    *What are the positive outcomes of this decision?*

2.    *How many positive outcomes are there?*

3.    *Are you able to prioritize the positive outcomes?*

4.    *What are the negative outcomes of this decision?*

5.    *How many negative outcomes are there?*

6.    *Are you able to prioritize the negative outcomes?*

7.    *How do the two sides stack up against each other?*

8.    *How do the prioritized sides stack up against each other?*

9.    *Is there a clear difference between the two columns?*

10.   *Are you still uncertain about your decision?*

# WORST CASE SCENARIO

In our earlier discussion, it was suggested that playing the "what if...." game was counter productive because the powers of imagination are very creative and the outcomes are not always realistic.

Sometimes, however, imagining the worst case scenario can be helpful, and tip a decision in the right direction. Counselors will often ask a client, " If you did this, what is the worst thing that could happen?" This technique sometimes shows us that what we fear most is actually not as bad as we thought, and it may relieve us of much guilt and worry.

Using the Balance Sheet technique mentioned above, you can develop another column next to the con side, where you evaluate the worst thing that could happen. In effect, you are exaggerating some of the items on the con side to see if they are really as bad as they appear to be.

The same approach can be adopted on the pro side, by asking the question: "If you did this, what is the best thing that could happen?" Here, the pro side may gain a little more weight.

Strangely, revealing the worst case scenario seems more powerful than the best case scenario. Since fear is a very strong and basic instinct, it may be that revealing the worst provides great relief.

## EXAMPLE

A budding sailor dreamed of sailing solo around the world in a yacht. He investigated the seaworthy yachts on the market but could not find one rugged enough or cheap enough for his modest income. He made a list of navigational and communication equipment that he needed, but it also proved to be too expensive. He struggled with the two decisions that were in many ways dependent on each other. The more rugged the yacht the less likely he would need emergency navigation and communication equipment. The more rugged the yacht the less equipment he would need. He made a list of the pros and cons but they seemed equally balanced. At last he decided to imagine the worst scenario that could befall him. He reasoned that if the yacht was swamped, the equipment would not really help him as he might be miles away from help. He might be able to signal his navigational coordinates, but if his yacht sank he doubted whether he could survive long enough to be rescued. He decided that he would wait until he could afford a rugged yacht and appropriate electronic equipment, rather than taking a chance.

## QUESTIONS

1.  *What is the worst thing that could happen?  Be careful of exaggeration.*

2.  *How do you feel about this negative outcome?*

3.  *Could you live with this negative  outcome?*

4.  *Who will be affected mostly in a negative way?*

5.  *If you cannot live with it, what alternatives do you have?*

6.  *What is the best thing that can happen?  Be careful of being overly optimistic.*

7.  *How do you feel about this positive result?*

8.  *Who will be affected mostly in a positive way?*

9.  *Is the worst scenario more powerful than the best scenario?*

# CONCLUSION

When Shackleton set out to explore the South Pole in the Endurance, he got stuck in the ice. Knowing that his ship was trapped and that the ice would eventually crush it's hull, he made a decision to abandon ship, leaving most of his supplies behind. The crew was not too happy with the decision, since they had to drag a small lifeboat along with them. They could take very few supplies and it was not long before they ran out of food and water. The desire to return to the ship was immensely strong. Crazed with hunger and thirst, they ploughed on until they reached a whaling station.

Was his decision a good one? It was a calculated risk for sure. There is no doubt that it was a costly decision as well, for many of the crew lost their lives. For those who survived (the majority of the crew) of course it was the right thing to do. Shackleton was regarded as a hero, but he felt heartsore about the crew members that did not make it. In retrospect, he did the right thing, but he had to accept a less than a perfect solution. He also had to deal with guilt associated with it.

Most leaders are put on a pedestal and expected to perform at a much higher level than they actually are able. Unrealistic expectations put tremendous pressure on them, but the myth that good leaders cannot make mistakes is bogus. No leader is ever perfect, and we are actually setting them up to fail if we believe they are. In my opinion, it is better for leaders to admit that they can and do make wrong decisions, than to pretend that they don't. Such admissions actually restore their credibility, they do not destroy it.

Just as leaders make decisions of profound significance, so we make decisions every day of our lives. No one is exempt from decision making, it is part of being human. As we have seen, the ability to make decisions is a wonderful gift, but it seems that there are two temptations: first, to underestimate the significance of our decisions (trivializing them), and second, to overestimate them (becoming overwhelmed by them). The ability to balance these extremes can be cultivated over time. We need to put them into perspective. The same applies to accountability. Though we cannot be held accountable for all of our decisions, we can be held accountable for some. Whether we like it or not, society generally holds us accountable for major or critical decisions! Owning our responsibility is a mature thing to do, but we need to learn to balance responsibility as well. To shrug off inappropriate responsibility, or blame, is healthy. To own appropriate responsibility is mature.

Since no one is perfect, it is obvious that we will make many mistakes or wrong decisions in the course of our lives. I believe mistakes are not bad in themselves, if we recognize what we have done and take steps not to repeat our behavior next time. This process of learning involves, objectivity, analysis, planning and resolution. It is possible to accomplish the process on our own, but sometimes, we may need a little help from fellow travelers. Whoever we choose to help us needs to be honest and trustworthy. Feedback must be trusted to do any good, a truth many of us do not fully understand.

When and if we have learned from our mistakes, we must recognize the need to move on, to put the past behind us and try again. Many people are haunted by the past, to the degree that they paralyze themselves with guilt and regrets. Reliving these events does not really help us, it just adds salt to old wounds.

These stages in the decision making process are also reflected in most religions. Here, sins are confessed, forgiveness obtained, reconciliation occurs and new life is offered. Forgiveness cannot be manipulated or bought, it is a gift offered by God or human victims, and must be accepted by faith. One of our greatest problems is accepting the reality of the gracious gift of forgiveness. Guilt is a very serious problem today and cripples far more people than we recognize.

Sometimes, a decision will be right even if we feel uncomfortable about it. It is important to discover what degree of discomfort is acceptable to us and whether we can live with it. What we are talking about is the art of compromise. Many adopt an "all or nothing" approach to the outcomes of decisions, but sometimes the results may show a high success rate, which may not be shabby at all. We have to decide what success rate is satisfactory or acceptable to us. For example, instead of ninety percent, would eighty percent be acceptable? Perfectionism often causes us to accept nothing less than one-hundred percent, an accomplishment which is often totally unrealistic. The expectation that decisions must be perfect actually sets us up to fail. Success or failure in reaching goals can depend to a large degree on whether we have set goals at a reasonable level or not.

Some people make decision easily and quickly, but those who do, quite often regret them. People who struggle to make decisions, probably arrive at better decisions, over time, provided they are not bogged down in self-doubt and a laborious process.

Why human's make the decisions they do, is not an easy question to answer. As we have seen, there are numerous internal and external factors that motivate us, some of which we are aware, others we are not. It is very important that we understand at least some of these factors, if we want to make good and satisfying decisions.

It is not realistic to expect that a person will use all of the approaches to decision making that are mentioned in this booklet. The reader should choose the check lists that are appropriate to their personality and background. Sometimes, however, we are not aware of the relevance of particular questions until we review them. If check sheets are used with the help of counseling, the counselor should recommend which ones will be most helpful.

The ultimate goal behind any assessments of this kind is satisfaction. Feeling happy and contented with a decision is a unique experience. Satisfaction is not easily come by in our consumer society which seems to thrive on dissatisfaction. Even if people are satisfied with what they possess, and the decisions they have made to acquire it, there will always be voices that suggest that bigger and better options are out there.

We must recognize that the dream world of advertising is

actually unrealizable. It is fake, even though we buy into it believing that the newest innovation will convert us from toads into princes!

In the Christian Scriptures, Jesus taught a parable about decision making. He said that a man was going overseas and so he divided his business into several sections. The owner gave some employees more responsibility than others. When he came back, he reviewed the progress of each section. The section head with the most responsibility had done very well, he had tripled his income. The section head with less responsibility had also done well, he had doubled his income. The section head with the least responsibility had done nothing, because he was afraid of risking his investment. Of the three heads, it was the last that was reprimanded by the owner because he was afraid to take any initiative and had decided to do nothing.

When this scripture is interpreted much emphasis is sometimes laid on the inequality of the assignments, but really the emphasis should be placed on what each man decided to do with what he got.

What we make of our lives is up to us. We have to make the decisions. We must seize the opportunities that present themselves or not. Depending on the circumstances, some may have more opportunities than others and will do better than others. Unfortunately, life is not fair and it is easy to become disillusioned about it, but we must do our best with what we have. It is not how much we have been given that matters, but what we decide to do with it. Of course there is an element of risk involved in the decision. Risk may be uncomfortable to us, but "nothing ventured, nothing gained" as the saying goes. Our maturity and development is probably more important that our safety or comfort. If we decide to do nothing, we have made a decision, and we will never know what could have been. Clearly we will feel better about our decisions, if we are informed and recognize what factors are influencing us.

# BIBLIOGRAPHY

**Introduction**
1.. McClusky, Tom, Sharpe, Michael, and Marriott, Leo. <u>Titanic and Her Sister Ships</u>. London: PRC Publishing Ltd., 1998. p 283-329

2. Harris, Robert. "Introduction to Decision Making." Virtual Salt, July 2, 1998 http://www.virtualsalt.com/crebook5.htm

3. Parrado, Nando, and Rause, Vince. <u>Miracle in the Andes: 72 Days on the Mountain and My Long Trek Home</u>. Random House Inc., 2007

**The Wonder of Decision Making**
4. Genesis:3, <u>Holy Bible: Revised Standard Version</u>. London: Oxford Press, 1963

5. "Attribution Theory"
Http://www.changingminds.org/explanations/theories

6. "*The Buck Stops Here*" Sign. Harry S. Truman Library and Museum, October 2, 1945

7. Matthews, Mitford. M., ed., *A Dictionary of Americanisms on Historic Principles*. Chicago: University of Chicago Press, 1951 pages 198-199

8. Roesch, S.C. and Amirkham, J.H. "Boundary conditions for self serving." 1997

9. "Personal Goal Setting." http://www.mindtools.com
E-book and Worksheet Pack. London: Mind Tools Ltd.
http://opus1journal.org/others/killerapps/paralysis.html

10. Truman and the Bomb: A Dictionary History edited
"The Decision to Drop the Atomic Bomb." Documents, 1945.
Harry S. Truman Library and Museum

11. "Decision Making skills"
Http://www.mindtools.com/pages/main/newMN_TED.htm

12. "Abraham Lincoln and George B. McClellan."
http://www.abrahamlincolnsclassroom.org/Library

13. Rafuse, Ethan S. McClellan's War: The Failure of
Moderation in the Struggle for the Union. Indiana Press, 2005

14. "Lyndon Baines Johnson 36th President of the USA"
Http://www.lnstar.com

15. "Vietnam War"
Http://www.wikipedia.org

16. Noelle-Neumann, Elizabeth. The Spiral of Silence. University
of Chicago Press, 1980

17. Martin J., and Peters K. "Survey of Communication Theory:
Spiral of Silence" University of South Carolina, 1999.

18. "Opposition to the Iraq War"
Http://www.wikipedia.org/wiki/opposition_to_the_Iraq_War

**Internal and External Factors**
19. "Psycho Analysis: The Psychodynamic Approach"
Http:// psychology.about.com/od/history of psychology

**Fear of Making a Mistake**
20. McClusky, Tom, Sharpe, Michael, and Marriott, Leo. <u>Titanic and Her Sister Ships</u>. London: PRC Publishing Ltd., 1998. p 336-360

21. Revised Standard Version of the Holy Bible. London. Oxford University Press, 1963, Psalm 51:1-17 and 1 John 1:5- 9

22. Ortberg, John. "The Porcupine's Dilemma." <u>Everybody's Normal Til You Get to Know Them</u>. Grand Rapids: Zondervan, 2003

23. Ortberg, John. "Put Down Your Stones" in <u>Everybody's Normal Til You Get to Know Them</u>. Grand Rapids: Zondervan, 2003

24. Http://www.Nasa.Gov/Columbia/home

**Paralysis of Decision Making**
25. "Choice Paralysis"
http://opus1journal.org/others/killerapps/paralysis.html

26. Howe, Carl D., Butt, Joseph L., Timmons, Mary C. "The Tyranny of Too Much Choice," June 1, 2004
http://blackfriarsinc.com/totm.html

**Not to Decide is to Decide**
27. "Final Solution"
http://www.mtsu.edu/~baustin/finlsol.html

28. http://www.september11news.com/

29. Tyre, Larry. The Father of Spin: Edward L. Bernays and the Birth of P. R. Http://wwwprwatch.org/prwissues

30. Noelle-Neumann, Elizabeth. The Spiral of Silence. University of Chicago Press, 1980

31. Http://www.BBC.Co.UK World News: "Freedom for Nelson Mandela." 11th February, 1990

32. Http://www.BBC.Co.UK World News: "Nelson Mandela-a Humanitarian." 14th August, 2001

33. Http://www.BBC.Co.UK World News: "Special Report: Truth and Reconciliation. F.W. de Klerk: Overseer of transition." 30th October 1998

**Rational Check Sheet**
34. Http://www.conservative-resources.com/definition-of-bias.html
35. Http://www.logical-fallacies.info "Logical fallacies: An Encyclopedia of Errors of Reasoning"

36. Http://www.sjsu.edu/depts/itl/7/part3/general.html Mission Critical (Fallacious Generalizations)

37. ABC News. "The Psychology of Stereotypes Http://ABC.news.go.com/2020/story?id=2442521&page=1

38. "International Online Training Program on Intractable Conflict: Inaccurate and Overly Hostile Stereotypes." Http://www.colorado.edu/conflict/stereotypes

**Family Check Sheet**
39. "Beliefs, Values and Practices" Http://www.attachmentacrosscultures.org/beliefs/index.html

40. "Children's involvement in family decision making." Joseph Rowntree Foundation, July 2005 - Ref 0365 http://www.jrf.org.uk/knowledge/findings/socialpolicy/0365.asp

**Culture Check Sheet**
(See Reference #39 above)

41. http://en.wikipedia.org/wiki/Culture

42. http://en.wikipedia.org/wiki/Culture_shock

43. http://edweb.sdsu.edu/people/CGuanipa/cultshok.htm

44. Siasoco, R.V., Ross, S. "Japanese Relocation Centers."
Http://infoplease.com

**Religion Check Sheet**
45. Brunner, Emil. "The Divine Calling." The Divine Imperative:
A Study in Christian Ethics
Cambridge: Lutterworth Press, 2003.

46. Ortberg, John"Discerning the Call." If You Want to Walk on
Water, You've Got to Get Out of The Boat. Grand Rapids:
Zondervan, 2000

**Ethical Check Sheet**
(See Reference #45 above)

47. "Ethics." The Internet Encyclopedia of Philosophy
http://www.utm.edu/research/iep/e/ethics.htm

48. "Goodness without God"
http://www.answers.com/topic/secular-humanism

**Emotional Check Sheet**
49. "Basic Emotions."
Http://changingminds.org/explanations/emotions/basic%20emotio
ns.htm

50. "Emotions"
http://changingminds.org/explanations/emotions/emotions.htm

**Consequences Check Sheet**
51. "What is Cause and Effect?"
http://www.cameron.edu/~carolynk/cause-effect.html

52. Palina, Steve. "Cause and Effect vs. Intention Manifestation,"
October 17, 2005
http://www.cameron.edu/~carolynk/cause-effect.html

**Goal-Setting Check Sheet**
53. "Tips on How to Set Attainable Goals for Yourself"
http://www.revolutionhealth.com
(See reference #9 above)